WHAT PEOPLE EARN

Peter Cappelli is a graduate of Cornell University and has worked for many years as an economic journalist. He is currently a Guest Scholar of the Brookings Institution in Washington DC and a Fulbright Scholar at Nuffield College, Oxford, where he is involved in research into wages and salaries.

Peter Cappelli

What People Earn

The Book of Wages and Salaries 1981

Macdonald & Co Publishers

A Futura Book

First published in Great Britain by
Macdonald & Co Publishers Ltd
London and Sydney

Copyright © Macdonald & Co Publishers Ltd

Limp edition: ISBN 0 7088 2121 9
Cased edition: ISBN 0 354 04710 8
Printed in Great Britain by
Richard Clay (The Chaucer Press) Ltd,
Bungay, Suffolk

Macdonald & Co Publishers Ltd,
Paulton House,
8 Shepherdess Walk,
London, N1 7LW

Contents

Introduction

1	Government Employees	15
2	Medical, Hospital and Allied Jobs	41
3	The Professions and Allied Jobs	51
4	Writers, Artists, Entertainers and Sportsmen	73
5	Hotel, Catering and Domestic Trades	91
6	Office, Clerical and Allied Jobs	99
7	Tradesmen and Manual Workers	127
8	Others	165
9	Hours	193
10	Perks and Benefits	197
11	Regional Pay Variations	205
12	Are Men Paid More?	207
13	Are The Old Paid Less?	217
	Appendix 1 How Weekly Wages Compare	221
	Appendix 2 Sources of Household Income	229
	Appendix 3 1924 v 1980 Wages Compared	231
	Index	233

Introduction

'It is better to have a permanent income than to be fascinating.'

Oscar Wilde

What people earn is still one of the obsessions of our society. Wages and death seem the only two subjects which people are unwilling to discuss and yet whether it be the salary of Margaret Thatcher (£36,725 of which £8,900 is voluntarily waived) or the stipend of a Roman Catholic Priest (about £8 per month) the subject is of unending interest. Not all of us can get a job like Paul McCartney's (estimated earnings £25,000,000 in 1980) but many could be farm labourers — but would we at £57.10 per week? One thing is certain — what people earn was an endless source of speculation until the arrival of this book.

We all know that wages and salaries are the payments made in return for the performance of labour services, but what counts as a labour service can be a difficult question — everything from the fitting of pipes by a plumber to a film star's personal appearances. Different jobs come with different rates of pay, but it is almost impossible to judge actual earnings from contracted rates. There are a number of special arrangements at the workplaces — bonuses, overtime, piecework, etc. — which cannot be estimated in advance but add to pay. Newspaper printers have a contract that sets out a weekly rate of about £80, but the Government's New Earnings Survey shows that these special arrangements brought earnings to twice that — £159.40. A manager may be on a salary of £10,000, but his actual compensation includes bonuses and perks — such as a free car and an expense account. Jobs advertising the same rate of pay may in fact yield quite different earnings, so it is important to set out actual earnings, which is what we try to do here. It does, however, remain irrefutable that the best predictor of a person's income is their occupation.

Of course, every job has its own character which determines whether it is interesting, difficult or pleasant to do. People look at these characteristics along with rate of pay to decide whether a job is worth taking. Is it better than the other things I could be doing? Because people's tastes differ, their judgements about which jobs are "worth it" will also differ. A certain few who love the sea and its sense of danger, might actually enjoy working on an oil rig and would take a job there even if it did not pay well. To get more than those few, however, employers have to pay more — substantially more to get people like me out there. The job becomes more attractive as the rate of pay rises, and more people would judge it as worth taking.

The same is true for those jobs that require costly training or special skills. People judge the pay and conditions against the necessary training to see whether that career is worth pursuing. Governments often try to attract students into socially useful careers by reducing the costs of acquiring the necessary training, through grants and stipends.

Skilled jobs generally do have higher pay, but there is nothing about skill per se that must command a higher wage. Employers pay what they have to pay in order to attract workers with the necessary skills. In the 19th and 20th centuries, the relative wage necessary to attract skilled clerical workers fell – sometimes below the level for unskilled manual work – because the expansion of compulsory education made it easy to obtain the basic training for clerical work.

Given workers' judgements and initial preferences towards jobs, employers raise wages to attract more workers into a job. How high the wages go, therefore, depends on how many workers are hired. And that depends on judgements made by employers as to the value that each additional worker contributes to his operations. An increase in that value, and employers want to hire more, but to attract more workers, they have to pay more. When oil was discovered in the North Sea, petroleum engineers became much more valuable and companies wanted to lure more of them away from someone else, and that could only be done by raising salaries. In a few years, these high wages should draw more students into petroleum science, and the shortage should ease.

These market forces clearly play an important role in determining wages and salaries. Still one can get the feeling that wage differentials are all based on voluntary decisions about careers, that one can choose any job simply by undertaking the right training and by altering one's tastes. But markets rarely operate smoothly. People often lack the necessary information to make accurate career choices, and they are not always free to change job and move to new areas in order to pursue better options. Natural talents, resources, and inclinations - as well as those acquired in our youth - limit our choice. Even though I would be willing to undercut substantially Cliff Richard's fee on his next concert, I doubt whether his producers would ignore the fact that I cannot sing and give me the contract.

Social forces also influence relative pay. An employer's demand for workers, for example, is exercised through his estimate of a given worker's value, and these estimates are quite subjective - often based on social conventions such as the increasingly suspect notion that men work harder than women. How workers assess a job's characteristics also depends on social attitudes and conventions. In addition, there are many jobs, particularly in managmenet, where the characteristics and the relevant training are unique to each employer. The salary structures tend to reflect career and status hierarchies rather than the type of market forces that I have described. The same general problem affects those parts of the public sector where output is not "priced". Here it is difficult to measure the value of output and workers' contributions. To get around this problem, employers often use salary surveys to see how much similar workers are receiving elsewhere.

Even where market forces are strong, workers are able to influence their own pay. It is interesting that for 500 years, since 1412, the relative pay of craftsmen and labourers in the building trades remained almost constant: craftsmen made 50 per cent more. This ratio acquired the force of custom and was applied as an accepted criterion in determining pay.

With the rise of trade unions, more workers have been able to participate in the setting of their own wages and there is little doubt that trade unions can raise the pay of their members relative to non-members. In Britain, the estimates are that unions have increased this relative wage by 22 - 31 per cent. Unions raise wages by controlling an employer's workforce to make certain that no-one can be hired below the union rate. Many would argue that professional organisations like the Bar are, essentially, unions that restrict entry in order to raise wages.

One thing that almost everyone recognises about wages and salaries is that they have risen over time. But so have prices. Prices have more than doubled since 1975, so that a pound now buys less than half what it did then. How much can one really buy with today's salary - what is its real value? We can estimate that by comparing wages against the price of a bundle of items that most people buy. The assumption is that the real value of that bundle is constant; the change in its price is caused by a decline in the purchasing power of the pound and is called inflation. By subtracting the inflation rate from the rate of increase in nominal pay - the figure on the pay stub - one can estimate whether the real wage has risen or fallen.

The wages and salaries presented here represent statistical averages of gross earnings per working week or year. Where these averages are not available, a range is presented which approximates the relevant average. It is important to remember that the actual variation in earnings within a given occupation is quite substantial. In part, this variation reflects differences between jobs that have the same title; a Branch Manager in a rural bank has quite different responsibilities than a Branch Manager in Lombard Street. Similarly, a high percentage of earnings in manual work is output-related (overtime, piecework, etc.) so that workers doing exactly identical jobs at the same wages rates might have different earnings depending on how busy their employer is. (This subject is covered in section 9.) Different earnings also reflect variations in the cost of living across the country. London workers have to earn more to compensate for the high cost of housing and transport. Many of the jobs listed in this book exist only in London - particularly those in finance. In general, the figures reported for white-collar work tend to be more representative of earnings in the London area, but the extent of wage variation by area is covered more fully in section 10.

A great difficulty with any data on earnings is that it becomes dated very quickly. For many jobs, earnings change week-by-week, partly because of output-related pay, but in addition, rates and salaries are adjusted once every year and sometimes more frequently. The figures for each occupation were taken from surveys and sampling not all of which were conducted at the same time in the calendar year. In general, though, we tried to set out the earnings figures that were prevailing as we enter 1981, and where this is not so we have given a date.

What one finds striking about these figures will depend on what one believed before reading them. Pay in Britain seems unique in at least one way, however. A substantial proportion comes in a form additional to basic rates. Overtime, shift premiums, and piecework earnings account for 25 per cent of manual's earnings. A comparable estimate is difficult to calculate for manage-ment, but a high percentage of total compensation comes in bonuses and perks. (I have dealt with these at the beginning of sections 6 and 7.) The group that benefits least from these arrange-ments seems to be clerical workers for whom perks are modest and output related earnings rare. One may also find that many of the jobs listed are unique to a given industry and not recognisable as an occupation (panel beaters in vehicle manufacture, for example).

Throughout this book, where basic minimums are mentioned there are references to a Wages Council appropriate for that job.

Wages councils are independent bodies that set statutory minimum wages for certain industries in Britain. The Councils are made up of three groups; employer representatives, worker repres-entatives, and independent members appointed by the Secretary of State. The group is chaired by one of the independent members. The worker's side presents the initial recommendations for increases which are debated by the Council. The independent members usually swing the balance in favour of a settlement. The final agreement on rates becomes known as the Statutory Minimum Remuneration – a combination of rates, overtime pay, and holiday arrangements which are legally enforceable. There is a Wages Inspectorate whose representatives are empowered to check on industries, making certain that the regulations of the Councils are being met.

There are 34 Wages Councils representing a total of 2.5 million workers. 80 per cent of those are in two industries; catering and retailing. The vast majority of workers covered are women – many are part-time or home workers. Earnings in these industries are very close to the statutory minimums. Where they are higher, the reason is likely to be substantial overtime hours.

I have tried in the text to group together jobs which have some relation to one another and put in the later sections and appendices information that is more relevant when a general idea of what people earn has been obtained. It is a source of endless fascination to pick out the anomalies and surprises, but on further inspection the similarities have their amusing side too. I was struck by the fact that a university teacher receives £6 per hour per pupil. A free-lance embalmer earns £6 per body!

CHAPTER ONE

Government Employees

TOP SALARIES IN GOVERNMENT

Salaries for the most important government jobs
are set by the Commons on recommendation from an
independent body — The Top Salaries Review Board
— chaired by Lord Boyle, who incidentally is not
paid for this work. The Board has the difficult
task of determining comparable pay for similar
jobs, or jobs with similar responsibility, in the
private sector. Its recommendations, based on the
comparability figures and other economic data,
are sent to the Commons which has the power to
amend them. The 1979 proposals, for example, were
implemented in a series of extended stages which
are to continue through 1981. At present, the
Commons is debating adjustments for 1981
salaries which would provide increases above the
figures shown (the 1979 proposals are still due
to be implemented).

PARLIAMENT   Rates Excluding Parliamentary Salary

	Proposed £ per year	Current £ per year
GOVERNMENT		
Prime Minister (Margaret Thatcher)	36,725	31,750

PARLIAMENT <u>Rates Excluding Parliamentary Salary</u>

	Proposed £ per year	Current £ per year
GOVERNMENT		
Lord Chancellor (Lord Hailsham)	44,500	35,200
Mr Speaker (George Thomas)	29,150	24,500
Cabinet Ministers (20 in all)	27,825	23,500
Ministers of State (26 in all)	19,775	16,250
Parliamentary Secretaries and Under Secretaries of State (30 in all)	15,100	12,350
Attorney General (Sir Michael Havers)	29,525	25,050
Solicitor General (Sir Ian Percival)	24,375	20,600
Lord Advocate (Lord Mackay of Clashfern)	27,875	20,600
Solicitor General for Scotland (Nicholas Fairburn)	20,925	17,150
HOUSE OF COMMONS		
Leader of the Opposition (Michael Foot)	25,550	20,950
Parliamentary Secretary to the Treasury (Chief Whip) (Michael Jopling)	23,225	19,300
Deputy Chief Whip (John Stradling Thomas)	19,775	15,500
Opposition Chief Whip (Michael Cocks)	19,775	16,250

Rates Excluding Parliamentary Salary

	Proposed £ per year	Current £ per year
Government Whips (5 in all)	12,775	10,250
Opposition Deputy Chief Whip (Walter Harrison)	12,775	10,250
Chairman, Ways and Means (Bernard Weatherill)	19,775	16,000
Deputy Chairman, Ways and Means (2 in all)	17,425	14,000
HOUSE OF LORDS		
Chief Whip (Lord Denham)	23,275	16,100
Deputy Chief Whip (Lord Sandys)	18,600	12,350
Government Whips (5 in all)	16,275	10,550
Opposition Chief Whip (Baroness Llewelyn-Davies)	16,275	9,950
Chairman of Committees	23,275	16,150
Principal Deputy Chairman of Committees	20,925	14,150
Leader of the Opposition in the House of Lords (Lord Peart)	18,600	11,900

Ministers Parliamentary Salary is £8130 and members of Parliament receive £12,000. There are 635 Members of Parliament in all. The salaries shown are those applicable for pension purposes. As last year, the Prime Minister and the Lord

Chancellor have decided to draw no more than the salary payable to other Cabinet Ministers (£27,825).

Perks: Allowance for secretary and part-time research assistant in Commons. Lords receive per diem allowances for subsistence, travel, and office expenditure (about £40 per day in all). Paid officers in the Lords receive a small allowance for secretarial help (£1,000 per year). There are 1,170 Peers eligible to sit in the House of Lords and to claim the allowances. The Prime Minister and Chancellor of the Exchequer have in addition a house each in Downing Street for which they do not pay rent. Tenure is however insecure.

SENIOR GRADES OF THE HIGHER CIVIL SERVICE

There are 24 Permanent Secretaries, 156 Deputy Secretaries and 578 Under-Secretaries.

	Proposed £ per year	Current £ per year
Head of the Home Civil Service (Sir Ian Bancroft) Permanent Secretary to the Treasury (Sir Douglas Wass) Secretary to the Cabinet (Sir Richard Armstrong)	35,845	33,500
Permanent Secretary	33,170	31,000
Second Permanent Secretary	30,495	28,500
Deputy Secretary	26,215	24,500
Under Secretary	21,935	20,500

CIVIL SERVANTS

Civil servants staff departments of the central government and are paid from funds approved by Parliament. There are over 500,000 non-industrial Civil Servants in clercial and administrative positions. Pay for Civil Servants is determined through a series of comparisons with similar work in the private sector, althoughrecently the government has tried to abandon this system. There is a Civil Service pay scale for every conceivable job - scientists, statistician, etc., - but the positions listed below are the general ones found in most departments.(The entry level grade for administrators is Executive Officer.)

	£ per year
Assistant secretary	14,250 - 17,000
Senior Principal	11,750 - 15,000
Principal	10,600 - 14,000
Senior Executive Officer	8,600 - 10,500
Higher Executive Officer	6,950 - 8,555
Higher Clerical Officer	5,790 - 6,745
Clerical Officer	3,688 - 4,740
Superintendent Of Typists	5,264 - 5,661
Senior Personal Secretary	4,728 - 5,894
Personal Secretary	4,123 - 4,980

Pay for the higher grades in the Civil Service is set by the Top Salaries Review Board.

INDUSTRIAL CIVIL SERVANTS

The government employs about 170,000 manual workers who are grouped together as the Industrial Civil Service. Most of these are employed in production operations of the Ministry of Defence. A small percentage of these are specialist grades (printers, technicians, etc.) whose pay closely follows that in the private sector. The following rates apply to everyone else – 98.95 per cent of industrial Civil Servants. The New Earnings Survey estimates that the average Industrial Civil Servant – across all grades – earns £99 per week.

	£ per week
Non-craftsmen	82.00
highest grade	110.00
Craftsmen (single grade)	108.00

The allowance is £19.46 per week for inner London and £8.12 for outer London. There is a special efficiency bonus payable of £5.00 per week.

NATIONALISED INDUSTRIES

	£ per year
British National Oil Corporation	
Chairman	53,500
(Lord Kearton)	
Deputy Chairman	36,250–45,000
Board member	29,250–37,750
British Steel Corporation	
(Mr Ian McGregor)	
Post Office	
Chairman	48,500
(Sir William Barlow)	
Deputy Chairman	34,500–42,000
Board member	28,500–34,500
Central Electricity Generating Board	
(Mr Glyn England)	
United Kingdom Atomic Energy Authority	
(Sir John Hill)	
Chairman	38,500
Deputy Chairman	27,500–33,500
Board member	22,750–27,500

£ per year

British Rail
(Sir Peter Parker)
British Gas Corporation
(Sir Dennis Rooke)
British Shipbuilders
(Admiral Sir Anthony Griffin)
National Coal Board
(Sir Derek Ezra)
British Airways Board
(Mr Ross Stainton)
British Aerospace
Dr A.W. Pearce)

	£ per year
Electricity Council	
Chairman	44,000
(Sir Francis Tombs)	
Deputy Chairman	29,250 − 35,750
Board member	23,250 − 28,750

Scottish Development
  Agency
National Bus Company
(Lord Shepheard)
National Freight
  Corporation
(Sir Robert Lawrence
and Mr V.G. Paige)
Civil Aviation Authority
British Airports Authority
(Mr N.I. Payne)

Cable and Wireless Ltd	
Chairman	31,000
Deputy Chairman	22,750 − 27,750
Board member	18,500 − 22,500

Regional Water	
Authorities − Chairman	22,250 − 27,750

Area Electricity Boards	
Chairman	22,250 − 26,500

	£ per year
Commonwealth Develop- ment Corporation	
North of Scotland Hydro- Electric Board	
South of Scotland Electricity Board	
Welsh Development Agency	
British Transport Docks Board	
Scottish Transport Group	
National Water Council	
Chairman	27,750
Deputy Chairman	20,000 - 24,500
Board member	15,750 - 19,750
British Waterways Board	
Chairman	18,000
Deputy Chairman	13,000 - 15,750
Board member	8,500 - 12,500

LOCAL AUTHORITY WORKERS
Manual

Local authorities are far and away the biggest single employer in Britain with 2.8 million workers. Those in education, the police, and the fire services have their pay determined through separate, independent negotiations; the rest bargain nationally as one group, with supplemental negotiations at lower levels. A high proportion of these workers are in low-skill jobs. The New Earnings Survey estimates that basic pay for local authority manual workers is £71 per week, £10.00 less than for industrial civil servants, and yet total weekly earnings in local authorities are slightly higher at £100.00 per week. The explanation is that payment-by-result schemes add £16 per week to local government pay. The following figures are basic rates for manual jobs in local government

as set out in the Clegg Commission recommendations. Actual earnings can be almost twice these
rates.

	£ per week
Cleaners	48.66
Labourers/kitchen assistants	49.60
School meals workers	51.12
Assistant gardeners/ assistant cooks	53.98
Car park attendants	54.45
Gardener/Pool attendant	56.20
Road workers/Drivers	59.08
Road workers/Drivers higher grades	61.58
Crematorium attendants	66.11

Clerical

The largest group of local authority workers is
however the clerical and professional grades.
Their salaraies are as follows:

Clerical Division	£ per year
Grade 1 - lowest	2,508 - 4,590
Grade 3 - Highest	5,148 - 5,574

Administrative, Professional Posts	
AP Grade 1 - Lowest	3,918 - 4,590
AP Grade 5 - Highest	6,870 - 7,338

Technicians and Technical Staff Division	
Grade 1 - Lowest	2,508 - 4,590
Grade 5 - Highest	6,870 - 7,338

Principal Officers	
Range 1 - Lowest	8,378 - 10,731
Range 2 - Highest	10,455 - 12,939

London allowance: inner London £915 per year;
outer London £483; inner fringe £237; outer
fringe £159. The hours of work are 36 per week in
London and 37 elsewhere.

FIRE SERVICE

There are over 60 fire brigades in Britain, and they employ close to 40,000 workers. The number of part time and volunteer workers approaches half that number again. Pay is set by collective bargaining through the local authority system. Because it is difficult to find comparison groups for comparability studies, the criterion for settlements tends to be general economic conditions – such as the cost of living and the overall rise in pay elsewhere. Overtime and shift premiums contribute about 8 per cent to actual earnings. The following rates include additional payments for unsocial hours, but exclude overtime and shift payments. If these were included, the average fireman would earn £118 per week.

	£ per week
Firemen (19 years and over)	85.00
During 3rd year of service	93.05
During 5th year (with qualifications)	106.39
Long serving (15 years) with qualifications	111.05
Leading firemen	113.92
Sub-officers (after one year)	121.28

A charge may be made where residential accommodation is provided. Firemen work 12-hour shifts, alternating between day and night shifts. The shifts are arranged so that the average number of hours worked in a week is 42. There is a London allowance of £543 paid annually.

POLICE

There are over fifty police forces in Britain, each administered by its own police authority (the Home Secretary for the Metropolitan Police). Trade union membership is prohibited as are strikes and other industrial action. Pay is negotiated through a Pay Negotiating Board consisting of government and police represent- atives and chaired by an independent member appointed by the Prime Minister. All but a very few matters are settled nationally. The rates quoted below exclude overtime payments which would raise pay about 13 per cent. With this included, the average Constable would earn £142 per week.

	£ per year
Constables	4,086
after 5 year's service	5,334
after 12 year's service	6,186
after 15 year's service	6,471
Sergeants	6,186
after 4 year's service	7,095
Station sergeants in London	7,479

There is a London weighting of £351 and a London allowance of £738 per year. Police authorities are also required to provide either free housing or an equivalent rent allowance. The annual allowance for dog handlers is £349 for Constables and £469 for higher grades.

	£ per year
Inspectors	8,880
after 4 years	9,774
Inspectors in London	9,072
after 4 years	10,242
Chief Inspectors	9,774 – 10,875
in London	10,242 – 11,340

PRISON OFFICERS

The New Earnings Survey estimates that the average Prison Officer (below the rank of principal) earns £191.07 per week. £75 of that comes from overtime pay. Basic rates for Senior Officers are 23 per cent above those for Prison Officers while those for Principal Officers are 37 per cent higher. All grades receive free uniforms. The London allowance is £11.46 to £14.95 per week for inner and £4.73 to £6.23 per week for outer London.

PROBATION OFFICERS

Supervise those placed under their care by the courts with the aim of rehabilitating offenders. Probation officers are employed by the Home Office.

	£ per year
Main Grade Officers	5,900 – 8,820
Senior Probation Officer	8,600 – 10,000
Assistant Chief Probation Officer	10,600 – 11,600

Chief Officer – varies with location. Up to £20,100 in inner London.

The London weighting is £483 for outer and £915 for inner London.

SOCIAL WORK

The term social work is a broad one, encompassing a range of skills directed towards aiding the economically underpriviledged and the socially maladjusted. Perhaps the best general description of the work is that it helps people to get along in their communities – economically and socially. The following list is by no means exhaustive, but it represents some of the more common job titles in social work. Most of these positions are in Metropolitan areas. Churches and religious groups occasionally employ social workers, but most are employed by county councils or London boroughs. These bodies have staff in other community-orientated positions.

Child-care Workers
Staff day-care centres and are responsible for pre-school children. Average earnings are around £5,500 per year.

Play Leaders
Responsible for the play activities of young children at a community or youth centre. Working hours will vary because of school holidays, etc., but are generally less than in child care. Pay is between £5,000-5,300 per year.

Senior Play Leaders
Supervise Play Leaders and direct activities at play centres. Pay is around £6,000 per year.

Youth Leaders
This job involves a good deal of counselling. Youth Leaders are responsible for teenage social activities at a community centre. Earnings vary between £6,000 and £8,000 per year depending on the size of the centre and the types of problems the youths are likely to have (areas where youth crime is a problem generally pay more).

Houseparents
Assist the staff at special schools for handicapped or disturbed children. The job usually involves monitoring the children outside regular staff hours. They earn about £4,200.

Family Social Workers
These positions handle casework; identifying a family's problems and bringing the appropriate

resources to bear. A good portion of this work involves determining the type of government aid that should be dispensed. They earn £6,700 – £7,100 per year.

Senior Social Worker
Supervises the casework being done by a staff of social workers. Pay varies with the size of the staff but averages about £8,000 – 8,200 per year.

Race Relations Advisor
Usually filled by a Senior Social Worker, a Race Relations Advisor identifies the special needs of a multi-racial community and provides advice on how to meet them. Pay is in line with that for Senior Social Workers (£8,000-8,200 per year).

Community Leisure Officer
The job that everyone thinks they would love, the Leisure Officer is generally responsible for adult recreation activities – usually athletics – at a community centre. Pay averages between £4,500 and £5,000 per year, but the job need not always be full-time.

Sports Coach
This position is almost always part-time and usually consists of teaching a particular sport or supervising games. Pay is about £2.50 per hour.

Training Officer
This position is on the same level as a Senior Social Worker and consists of designing and administering training programs to provide staff for a council or borough. Salaries are between £8,500 and £9,500 per year.

Occupational Therapists
These therapists provide rehabilitative activities for those who have been physically or

psychologically impaired. The idea is to get them
to function normally in the community. Therapists
operate under medical supervision. Earnings
average around £6,500, rising to £7,500 for those
with supervisory responsibilities.

Housing Manager
A Housing Manager administers blocks of flats for
an agency - such as a local council. They must
see that rents are paid as well as that necessary
maintenance is performed. Pay averages around
£7,500, depending on the number of flats.

CAREERS OFFICERS
Offer advice to school leavers and help place
them in employment. They are appointed and paid
by local authorities who have some discretion
where they begin on the local authority salary
scale. Careers Officers in inner London are paid
between £6,050 and £8,800 per year and the London
allowance is £980.

JUDICIARY
There are 22 Justices of Appeal and 98 High Court
Judges.

	Current £ per year	Proposed £ per year
Lord Chief Justice (Lord Lane)	40,000	44,500
Master of the Rolls (Lord Denning)	37,000	41,000
Lords of Appeal (18 in all)		
Lord President of the Court of Session (Scotland) (Lord Emslie)		

	Current £ per year	Proposed £ per year

Lord Chief Justice
  (Northern Ireland)
(Lord Lowry)
President of the Family
  Division
(Sir John Lewis Arnold)
	35,500	39,000

Lord Justice of Appeal
Lord Justice Clerk
  (Scotland)
(Lord Wheatley)
Lord Justice of Appeal
  (Northern Ireland)
	33,500	37,500

Vice-Chancellor	33,000	37,500

High Court Judge
Judge of the Court of
  Session (Scotland)
Puisne Judge (Northern
  Ireland)
	32,000	35,000

President, Lands Tribunal
  (England and Wales)
President, Transport
  Tribunal
Chief Social Security
  Commissioner (England,
  Wales and Scotland)
President, Industrial
  Tribunals (England and
  Wales)
	24,000	25,500

President, Industrial
  Tribunals (Scotland)
Sheriff Principal
  (Scotland)
	23,250	24,750

	Current £ per year	Proposed £ per year
Chairman, Scottish Lands Court	23,250	24,750
President, Lands Tribunal (Scotland)		
Official Referee (London)	22,500	24,500
Vice-Chancellor of the County Palatine of Lancaster		
Recorder of Liverpool		
Recorder of Manchester		
Senior Circuit Judge, Newington Causeway		
Recorder of Belfast (Northern Ireland)		
President of the Lands Tribunal (Northern Ireland)		
Chief Social Security Commissioner (Northern Ireland)		
Circuit Judge	22,000	23,250
Chief Metropolitan Magistrate		
Member, Lands Tribunal (England and Wales and Scotland)		
Social Security Commissioner		
Judge Advocate General		
Sheriff A (Scotland)		
County Court Judge (Northern Ireland)		
Master of the Court of Protection		
Senior and Chief Masters and Registrars of the Supreme Court		

	Current £ per year	Proposed £ per year
Registrar of Criminal Appeals	22,000	23,250
President, Industrial Tribunals (Northern Ireland)		
Member, Lands Tribunal (Northern Ireland)		
Social Security Commissioner (Northern Ireland)		
Regional Chairman, Industrial Tribunals (England, Wales and Scotland)	21,500	22,750
Chairman, Foreign Compensation Committee		
Sheriff B (Scotland)	21,500	23,250
Master and Registrars of the Supreme Court	19,500	20,750
Metropolitan Magistrate		
Chairman, Industrial Tribunals (England, Wales and Scotland)		
Vice-Judge Advocate General		
Provincial Stipendiary Magistrate		
Resident Magistrate (Northern Ireland)		
Chairman, Industrial Tribunals (Northern Ireland)		
Master, Supreme Court (Northern Ireland)		

	Current £ per year	Proposed £ per year
County Court Registrars and District Registrars of the High Court	19,250	20,500

ARMED FORCES

Pay in the Armed Forces is set by special review bodies; the Top Salaries Review Body sets salaries for the highest officers, while the Armed Forces Review Body determines the pay for everyone else. In both cases, the criteria are the same; cost of living increases and general economic factors tend to explain the overall level of the recommendations while differences in retention rates and responsibilities determine the pay changes between grades. This is one group where the pay scales are actually different for men and women.

SENIOR OFFICERS IN THE ARMED FORCES

	Current £ per year	Proposed £ per year
Admiral of the Fleet Field Marshal Marshal of the Royal Air Force	33,500	35,845
Admiral General Air Chief Marshall	31,000	33,170
Vice-Admiral Lieutenant General Air Marshal	24,500	27,000

	Current £ per year	Proposed £ per year
Rear Admiral Major General Air-Vice Marshal	20,500	21,935

ROYAL NAVY AND ROYAL MARINES
Normal Rates for Officers

£ per year

Captain R.N.	17,480 – 20,900
Colonel R.M.	20,900
Lt. Colonel R.M.	17,480
Commander R.N. Major R.M.	15,012 – 16,589
Lt. Commander R.N. Captain R.M.	11,304 – 13,494
Lieutenant R.N. Lieutenant R.M.	8,979 – 10.424

Sub-Lieutenant and R.M. Sub-
  Lieutenant after 3 years in
  rank
	5,950 – 7,789

Artificers, Mechanicians, Medical and Communications Technicians

These rates are to be increased by approximately 10.3% during the course of 1981.

	Minimum Per Day	Maximum Per Day
Mechanician Technician (Able)	13.85	14.60
Artificer	16.03	16.78
Mechanician Technician (Leading) Mechanician/Medical Technician (Leading)	17.01	17.76

	Minimum Per Day	Maximum Per Day
Mechanician/Medical Technician (Petty Officer)	19.00	19.75
Artificer (Acting Petty Officer)		
Artificer Mechanician Technician (Chief Petty Officer)	19.93	24.15
Chief Artificer/ Mechanician/ Technician	24.10	24.85
Fleet Chief Petty Officer	24.70	25.45

Other Branches

	£ per year
Ordinary Rating	4,084 – 6,085
Able Rating	4,960 – 6,774
Leading Rating	6,033 – 7,563
Petty Officer	6,986 – 8,205
Chief Petty Officer	7,424 – 9,391
Fleet Chief Petty Officer	7,888 – 10,348

ROYAL MARINES
General Duties, Tradesmen and Musicians

	£ per year
Marine 2nd Class	4,084 – 6,085
Marine 1st Class	4,960 – 6,774
Corporal	6,033 – 7,563
Sergeant	6,986 – 8,205
Colour Sergeant	7,424 – 9,391
Warrant Officer	7,888 – 10,348

WOMEN'S ROYAL NAVY

These rates are to be increased by approximately 10.3% during the course of 1981.

	£ per year
3rd Officer	4,964 – 6,669
2nd Officer	7,508 – 8,720
1st Officer	9,552 – 11,450
Chief Officer	12,468 – 13,811
Superintendent	14,939 – 16,560
Director	18,049

ARMY

	£ per year
Brigadier	20,900
Colonel	17,480 – 19,319
Lt. Colonel	15,012 – 16,589
Major	11,304 – 13,494
Captain	8,979 – 10,424
Lieutenant	7,220 – 7,979
Second Lieutenant	5,950

Royal Army Veterinary Corps

These rates are to be increased by approximately 10.3% during the course of 1981.

	£ per year
Captain, Major and Lieutenant Colonel	
On Entry	8,497
After 27 years	15,067

Colonels and Brigadiers are paid at the same rate as their equivalent ranks who are not specialised.

Quartermaster

These rates are to be increased by approximately 10.3% during the course of 1981.

	£ per year
Lieutenant, Captain, and Major	9,749 – 11,275
Lieutenant Colonel	12,706 – 12,888

Chaplains

These rates are to be increased by approximately 10.3% during the course of 1981.

	£ per year
Captain, Major and Lt. Colonel	
On Entry	7,866
After 26 years	14,242
Chaplain General	18,250

Other Ranks

The other ranks in all the armed forces are paid on a scale according to the number of years for which a recruit commits himself to serve and a seniority rating within that scale. These are the maxima and minima for each rank:-

	£ per year
Private	4,084 – 6,085
Lance Corporal	4,960 – 6,774
Corporal	6,033 – 7,563
Sergeant	6,986 – 8,205
Staff Sergeant	7,424 – 9,391
Warrant Officer	7,888 – 10,348

WOMEN'S ROYAL ARMY CORPS

These rates are to be increased by approximately 10.3% during the course of 1981.

	£ per year
Officer Cadet	3,500
Second Lieutenant	4,964
Lieutenant	6,026
Captain	7,508
Major	9,552
Lieutenant-Colonel	12,468
Colonel	14,939
Brigadier	18,049

ROYAL AIR FORCE
Officers

	£ per year
Pilot Officer	5,950
Flying Officer	7,220 – 7,979
Flight Lieutenant	8,979 – 10,424
Squadron Leader	11,304 – 13,494
Wing Commander	15,012 – 16,589
Group Captain	17,480 – 19,319
Air Commodore	20,900

Airmen

These rates are to be increased by approximately 10.3% during the course of 1981.

	Minimum Per Day		Maximum Per Day
Air Crew Cadet	10.06	–	17.28
Air Electronics Operator and Air Engineers	10.06	–	17.28
Air Loadmasters	10.06	–	17.58
Pilots, Navigators, Air Electronics Operators and Air Engineers			
Sergeant	19.93	–	20.68
Flight Sergeant	23.24	–	23.99
Master Aircrew	24.70	–	25.45

	Minimum Per Day	Maximum Per Day
Air Signallers and Air Loadmasters		
Sergeant	18.40	19.15
Flight Sergeant	21.50	22.25
Master Aircrew	22.96	23.71

WOMEN'S ROYAL AIR FORCE

These rates are to be increased by approximately 10.3% during the course of 1981.

	£ per year
Officer Cadet	3,500
Pilot Officer	4,964
Flying Officer	6,016
Flight Lieutenant	7,508
Squadron Leader	9,552
Wing Commander	12,468
Group Captain	14,939

GOVERNMENT SCIENTISTS

Scientists working for the central government are involved in a wide variety of areas, from operations research to the physical and life sciences. Like other civil servants, their pay is determined through a process of pay research — comparisons with other grades in the Civil Service or with similar work elsewhere. The latter argument seems to be winning despite the difficulty in finding the appropriate comparisons. This year's settlement came in the form of an arbitration award.

	£ per year
Assistant Scientific Officer	3,605 – 4,999
Scientific Officer	4,809 – 6,480

£ per year

	£ per year
Higher Scientific Officer	6,075 – 7,999
Senior Scientific Officer	7,644 – 9,619
Principal	9,690 –12,540
Senior Principal	14,706 –16,250

NEW TOWNS STAFF

These employees handle the planning and development of New Towns. They are government employees, and their ranks include a number of professionals – urban planners and architects in particular.

£ per year

	£ per year
Clericals	2,500 – 4,400
Technical grades (lowest)	4,450 – 4,850
(highest)	4,950 – 5,500
Administrative grades (lowest)	5,620 – 6,150
(highest)	8,880 – 9,575
Upper salary range (professionals, etc.)	12,700 –13,500
Upper salary range highest grade	15,200 –16,200

The hours of work are 35 and the London allowance is £1,016 per year for the upper salary range and £726 elsewhere.

CHAPTER TWO

Medical, Hospital and Allied Jobs

DOCTORS AND DENTISTS

Pay for doctors and dentists is set by a Review Body and is based largely on the general movement of earnings in the economy and its distribution. The idea is that doctors and dentists should maintain their relative position in the pay heirarchy. Very few doctors or dentists are on a straight salary, however. Most have a practice and are paid a fee for each job that they perform. Their earnings vary with the number of patients they see and the type of treatment they give. Of course, there are private as well as National Health Service patients, and this additional practice adds about 10% to earnings in the medical and dental professions. It is not unusual for practitioners in the London area to double their income through private practice.

	£ Per Year
House Officers	5,400–6,100
Senior House Officers	6,700–7,600
Registrars	7,600–9,260
Senior Registrars	8,770–11,220

	£ per year
Consultants	15,510–19,870
Senior Hospital Medicals and Dental Officers	15,510
Medical Assistants and Assistant Dental Surgeons	9,450–15,510

General Practioners will have a guaranteed income of £21,175. In practice this comes as a series of allowances and capitation fees, some of which are listed below. Of course, they can earn more.

Standard capitation fee (the fee for each patient on a G.P.'s list).

	£ per year
Patients Under 65	4.15
Patients 65 and Over	6.54
Night Visit Fee	10.50
Vaccinations	1.60 – 4.50
Treatment of a Fracture	9.00

Dental Practitioners, the Review Body estimates, will find that their average net income is around £14,750. The sessional fee per hour is £7.10 for dental surgeons and £11.50 for consultants.

The most recent data from the Inland Revenue produces the following distribution of professional incomes for doctors and dentists. This distribution only includes income received from the practice of medicine and dentistry, respectively. There are some people who listed their profession as Doctor or Dentist yet do not practice – either retired or earning their living through other means. And this accounts for the large percentage of Doctors and Dentists who earn almost nothing from their practices.

Even these figures — which are the most recent ones — are three years old. If professional earnings increased at the same rate as those in the rest of the economy, they would be 30 — 40 per cent higher in 1980 than the figures listed below.

Earnings £	Doctors Practising as Individuals	Practising in Partnership
	%	%
Nil	28	2.6
500	10	0.7
1,000	7.8	0.1
1,500	6.2	0.8
2,000	9.4	1.2
3,000	6.2	1.3
4,000	5.5	1.4
5,000	4.6	1.6
6,000	4.3	1.1
7,000	3.9	1.2
8,000	3.5	1.8
9,000	2.8	1.7
10,000	3.5	3.2
12,000	1.8	6.6
15,000	1.3	10.9
20–100,000	0.8	63.5

	Dentists Practising as Individuals	Practising in Partnership
	%	%
Nil	9.6	10
500	3.7	10
1,000	3.5	10
1,500	4.1	1.3
2,000	6.7	3.0
3,000	6.3	3.0
4,000	8.8	2.8
5,000	10.3	1.0

	Dentists Practising as Individuals	Practising in Partnership
	%	%
6,000	8.6	1.8
7,000	8.3	3.6
8,000	5.7	1.8
9,000	5.9	4.1
10,000	7.4	5.0
12,000	5.9	8.0
15,000	3.2	14.3
20-100,000	1.9	43.0

Quite clearly, practicioners in partnerships have higher professional incomes. The reason, it would seem, is that only those with a full-time commitment to the practice are likely to be in partnerships; those not practicing or doing so only part-time are unlikely to find places in partnerships where work loads tend to be higher.

DENTAL TECHNICIANS

	£ per year
Student Technicians (age 16)	2,420-2,568
(Age 23 and over)	3,417-3,552
Technicians	4,404-5,790
Chief Technicians I	6,291-7,203
Chief Technicians II	6,894-7,845

There are special payments for emergency duty; £5.50 for periods spent on 'standby' and £3.93for 'on-call' duty. The London allowance is £527 per year for inner and £141 for outer London.

NURSES/MIDWIVES

The determination of nurses' and midwives' pay was turned over to the Clegg Commission and recommended increases were issued early in 1980. Most midwives are Registered Nurses, and therefore they have no separate scale.

	£ per year
Regional Nursing Officers	12,629 – 16,815
Area Nursing Officers	10,721 – 15,948
District Nursing Officers	8,247 – 14,670
Senior Nursing Officers	5,704 – 6,942
Nursing Officers	5,351 – 6,391
Sisters	4,698 – 6,195
Staff Nurses	3,715 – 4,530
Enrolled Nurses	3,346 – 4,036
Nursing Auxilliaries/ Assistants	2,507 – 3,209
Student Nurses	2,747 – 3,000

Perks: Nurses receive premium rates for unsociable hours.

INDUSTRIAL MEDICAL OFFICERS/

Occupational Physicians are the 'company doctors' whose special concern is with occupational disease and accidents. A great number of these positions are part-time so that multiple appointments are quite common. The British Medical Association publishes guidelines for the pay of Industrial Medical Officers which are based on the report of the Review Body on Doctors' and Dentists' Remuneration. The various grades reflect differences in qualifications and experience.

Full-time Positions

	£ per year
Occupational Physician (lowest grade)	9,470 – 12,120
Occupational Physician (higher grade)	11,060 – 17,690
Senior Physicians	15,510 – 19,870
Chief Physicians	23,400 (minimum)

Part-time Positions

Hours Per Week	£ per year
0-1	648 - 894
1-2	1,222 - 1,689
5 sessions per week	7,188 - 9,936
9 sessions per week	12,939 - 17,883

(Sessions average 2 hours each.)

Company Nurses
The pay for company nurses is based on the prevailing rates for similar work in the National Health Service.

	£ per year
Occupational Health Nurses	4,746
Officers	5,034 - 8,298
Senior Officers	7,245 -10,512
Chief Officers (administration)	9,204 -12,036

PSYCHOLOGISTS
There are various types of psychologists but they all share the study of mental processes and their relationship to behaviour. Almost all are employed by the government; a large proportion in education. Educational psychologists specialise in the study and treatment of problems associated with children at school — especially learning disabilities. The following scales are basic salaries for educational psychologists which are part of the teacher's pay schedule. Actual earnings will be very close to these figures.

	£ per year
Assistants	5,300 - 6,300
Educational Psychologists	5,300 - 8,600
Senior Psychologists	8,500 - 9,700
Principal Psychologists	9,000 -11,000

Clinical Psychologists

Specialists in diagnosing and treating abnormalities — often the more severe kinds — in conjunction with a medical doctor. They are employed by the NHS, and their top salary grade is just over £11,000 per year.

Occupational Psychologists

Study the problems related to work. They are involved in training, testing, and personnel selection. In the private sector, they are often employed as consultants by a company's personnel department. Occupational psychologists are, in general, better paid than other psychologists, primarily because of this demand from the private sector where salaries average between £10,500 — £11,500 per year. They can go much higher, however, especially for those consulting in a number of firms.

AUXILIARY MEDICAL PROFESSIONS

This group of professions is paid on a common scale given overleaf.

Chiropodist

Diagnoses and treats ailments of the foot.

Occupational Therapist

Works to improve the abilities and general independence of those who are disabled.

Physiotherapist

Works to aid the reovery of physical disabilities through massage, exercise, and so on.

Remedial Gymnast

Instructs patients in gymnastic activities designed to improve the workings of the body and limbs.

Radiographer
Operate X-ray and other nuclear devices for diagnostic and therapeutic purposes.

Dietitian
Plans, instructs and advises on therapeutic diets.

Speech Therapist
Assists patients in overcoming speech disorders.

All these health professionals are paid on the same scale:-

	£ per year
Basic Grade	3,800-4,500
Senior II	4,700-5,533
Senior I	5,533-6,200
Superintendent III	6,200-6,867
Superintendent I	7,700-8,600
Teaching Grades:	
Teacher	6,400-7,134
Principal	8,000-8,900

Orthoptist
Instructs patients in exercises to improve muscle defects of the eye.

	£ Per Year
Basic Grade	3,800-4,500
Senior II	4,700-5,533
Head II	5,533-6,200
Head I	6,200-6,867
Teaching Grades:	
Teacher	6,400-7,134
Principal	8,000-8,900

AMBULANCEMEN
Give first-aid and transport the injured and infirm to treatment. Britain has 17,000 ambulancemen employed by the NHS. The following

are basic rates for a 40-hour week. Those 40 hours count not just time on the road but also time waiting for calls.

	£ per week
Leading Ambulancemen	83.00
Qualified Ambulancemen	76.50
Attendant	67.00
Attendant Single Manning	62.75

Special shift payments and overtime contribute substantially to earnings. Standby duty on Sundays and holidays, for example, earns a premium of £40 per day.

VETERINARY SURGEONS

Veterinarians diagnose and treat animal diseases. Only about half of Britain's practicing vets are in private practice. The rest are employed by universities – where they are paid according to lecturer rates – or by the Ministry of Agriculture and Fisheries. Fully qualified Vets in the Ministry earn a minimum of £9,694 per year, and the scale rises to £12,540. Those in private practice can probably earn more depending on the location of the practice and whether they are partners. The earnings of vets in such special circumstances as race horse stables obviously command a premium because of the value of the animals in their care.

CHAPTER THREE

The Professions and Allied Jobs

CLERGY

Church of England	£ per year	Number
Archbishop of Canterbury (Robert Runcie)	12,590	1
Archbishop of York (Stuart Blanche)	10,990	1
Bishop of London (Graham Leonard)	10,218	1
Bishop of Durham (John Habgood)	8,980	1
Bishop of Winchester (John Taylor)	7,442	1
Diocesan Bishops	8,060	38
Suffragan Bishops	6,565	61
Full-time Assistant Bishops	6,300	4
Deans and Provosts	6,565	41
Archdeacons	4,730	
Residentiary Canons	5,300	83
Incumbents	4,301	7,340
Chaplains and clergymen in non-parochial posts	4,364	
Assistant curates	3,542	
Deaconesses	3,633	

Perks: The estimated value of 'in kind' benefits for clergymen is £2,450 and comes almost entirely in the form of the use of a house with insurance, rates, and repairs provided. The Church also provides funds to meet working expenses of the clergy — covering all the expenses of diocesan bishops, for example, and an average of £687 per year for Incumbents, many of whom pay a substantial proportion of expenses themselves. The Church also provides pensions which range from 50 per cent of Incumbent's income to 27 per cent for the Archbishop of Canterbury who, in addition, gets the use of Lambeth Palace. The two Archbishops and twenty-four of the Diocesan Bishops also sit in the House of Lords.

Unitarian and Free Churches		£ per year
	Ministers' Full Scale	Associate Scale	Lay Pastor Scale
Year 1 & 2	2,680	2,530	2,380
			2,480
3	2,885	2,735	2,580
4	3,007	2,857	2,680
5	3,130	2,980	2,680
6	3,281	3,131	2,885
7	3,439	3,289	3,007
8	3,598	3,448	3,130
9	3,763	3,613	3,281
10	3,929	3,779	3,439
15	4,000	–	–

Associated Ministers are those whose responsibility to their congregation is less than full time. Those who spend a proportion of their time in their ministry receive that proportion of the Associate Minister rate. Associate Ministers working full-time in the ministry would receive the full Associate rate rather than the Minister rate, because the situation is expected to be temporary and because the long-term commitments of the two groups are different. Lay Pastors almost always have an outside source of income, and their time commitment to a congregation is even less than an Associate Minister.

Perks: Housing allowance - £950 per year in the provinces, £1,425 in the London area or a residence provided with rates and rent free. Allowances for cars and for expenses are provided as well as the rent for the telephone. Finally, a contribution is made to the Ministers' Pension and Insurance Fund by the Church.

Baptists
The minimum salary for a Baptist Minister is £3,600 per year, but each church can establish its own rate above that minimum. The congregation must provide housing for its minister - either rent and rates or an allowance of £900 per year where the minister owns his home. Help with light, heat, and phone bills is expected, and all out-of-pocket expenses for church business should be met by the congregation. All Baptist churches contribute to a central fund from which the poorer churches draw to help pay their minister's salary.

Roman Catholics
Catholic priests receive a stipend of about £16.00 every two months. In addition, the Easter offering in each church goes to the priests. They can also accept small offerings for special masses, but this would rarely amount to more than a few pounds per week. Most dioceses provide cars or allowances to cover their operation. Accommodation, food, and laundry services are provided without charge.

Episcopal Church of Scotland

	£ per year
Bishops of:	
Abderdeen and Orkney	10,746
Argyll and Isles	9,207
Brechin	7,341
Edinburgh	8,948
Glasgow and Galloway	8,180
Moray, Ross, Caithness	7,950
St. Andrews, Dunkeld and Dunblane	7,565

All these bishops have use of a residence.

Wesleyan Reform Union

The minimum salary for full-time minister is £2,474 per year. Payments above that rate depend on the income of the individual church. Rent and rates are paid by the church as are all reasonable expenses. Ministers pay their own light and heat bills.

Methodists

The average stipend is £3,975 per year for all full-time ministers. Those with less than 10 years service earn £3,855, the scale increasing with years in service.

United Reformed Church

Basic stipend for full-time Ministers.

	£ Per Year
Less than 10 years of service	3,074
Between 10 and 20 years	3,137
More than 20 years	3,200
Part-time (maximum)	2,214
Pulpit supply fees	£2.50–7.50 per service

Ministers receive allowances for their children (up to £140 per year for an older child) in addition to their stipend. Each church provides either free housing or a housing allowance and meets the cost of rates, heat and light. Where a car is essential the local church provides it and covers the operating expenses. The local church can pay stipends above the basic rates.

ARCHITECTS

Like other professions, architecture has private firms that are owned by partners — known as principals — who take their income as a percentage of the firm's receipts. While some partners are paid a salary, most of those on salaries are junior architects. Their relatively low pay in the hierarchy is explained in part by their lack of experience. In general, the older an architect and the larger his firm is, the higher his pay will be. But 40 per cent of all architects work in the public sector; 28 per cent for local authorities. They had the biggest increases this year, perhaps because their pay was based on the 'catch-up' recommendations of the Clegg Commission.

	£ per year	
	Median	Common Range
Private Practice Sole Principals	8,645	5,260 — 12,783
Private Practice Partners (excluding Sole Principals)	12,871	8,900 — 19,400
All Principals	11,650	7,500 — 17,700
Private Practice Salaried	7,600	6,500 — 8,900
Local Government	9,400	8,300 — 10,950
Central Government and National Boards	10,900	9,200 — 13,300
All other private employers, industries, etc.)	9,300	8,100 — 11,500

Inland Revenue has calculated the following distribution of earnings for Architects' professional incomes. These figures, although they are the most recently published, are three years old. Estimates put appropriate figures for 1980 about 35 per cent above these.

	%	Practicing in Partnerships %
Nil	3.6	12.2
500	9.8	0.6
1,000	8.2	2.5
1,500	4.6	1.8
2,000	10.3	3.7
3,000	9.5	3.3
4,000	5.6	2.4
5,000	2.2	2.2
6,000	3.1	2.8
7,000	2.7	2.0
8,000	1.3	2.3
9,000	1.3	2.2
10,000	1.8	4.6
12,000	1.8	5.3
15,000	1.5	8.8
20,000	–	25.5
50,000	0.7	9.2
100,000	–	8.5

The large number of architects with no professional incomes reflects not only those who have retired, but also those trained as architects who have taken up other jobs – some related to architecture.

BARRISTERS/SOLICITORS

Solicitors provide advice and handle legal problems for clients. Barristers function as consultants and advocates and plead cases on behalf of solicitors in the courts. The two professions are quite different and so is their training. They sit different exams and in addition barristers must serve one year's 'pupillage' for which they have to pay 100 guineas, whilst solicitors are required to serve from 2 to 4 years as 'articled clerks' for which they are modestly paid, perhaps £30 - £50 per week in London.

The average earnings for Barristers are just over £9,000 per year, but there is a tremendous range of earnings within the profession. Over 70 per cent of Barrister's are under the age of 40, many of them just setting out in the field and therefore qualified for only the simpler cases - which obviously yield low fees. Earnings for Barristers with more experience (those over age 40) average just under £19,000 per year. There is some evidence that those Barristers who are successful in their application for admission to the Queen's Council do earn more. In part, this may simply reflect their greater experience and be independent of the fact that they have taken silk, because doing so increases their costs. A QC requires a junior Barrister to appear with him or her in court). Salaried Barristers employed in industry or finance average around £17,000 per year.

There is also a great range of employment for Solicitors. Those working in industry average about £16,000 per year £12,600 for Legal Assistants and £24,000 for Senior Advisors. Those in partnerships average around £15,000, with principals earning about £17,500 and non-principals averaging about £13,000. Salaried partners earn about the same as non-salaried partners, but the variance in their earnings is significantly less. For non-salaried partners receive a share of the firm's profits and this may vary greatly between firms and within firms.

The Inland Revenue has constructed the following distributions of Barristers and Solicitors professional incomes. The information is however three year's old now, and estimates would place actual earnings for 1980 about 35 per cent above these figures used to calculte the distribution.

Barristers	Solicitors Not In Partnerships	Practicising in Partnerships
	%	%	%
Nil	12	25	4.1
500	7.3	8.3	0.6
1,000	7.7	5.8	0.5
1,500	6.4	4.7	0.4
2,000	9.0	6.8	1.1
3,000	6.9	6.6	0.6
4,000	8.5	6.5	0.7
5,000	6.0	3.4	2.2
6,000	6.6	5.0	1.5
7,000	4.3	4.7	0.7
8,000	4.6	3.7	0.9
9,000	3.9	2.8	0.8
10,000	4.0	5.3	2.7
12,000	4.9	4.2	3.2
15,000	3.5	3.3	7.6
20,000	4.3	3.9	33.0
50,000	4.3	3.9	22.2
100,000	4.3	3.9	17.7

The large percentage of Barristers reporting little or no professional income reflects both those who choose not to practice (retire or make a living through other means) and the oversupply of young Barristers which is inevitable when the long period required to establish oneself in the field is taken into consideration.

The large percentage of solicitors not in partnerships who report no professional income may best be explained by the relatively common practice in industry of hiring solicitors on a full-time basis to oversee particular aspects of operations. Income from such employment is not counted as professional income from the practice of law.

TAX CONSULTANTS

Tax consultants offer advice on which taxes apply in given situations as well as on ways to minimise tax liability.They are usually either qualified lawyers or accountants. These consultants are often self-employed, offering advice to individual clients for a fee. They are also employed on the staff of companies, particularly multi-national companies whose tax problems are prodigious. (For example, goods are often manufactured in one country, assembled in another, and sold in a third. Which taxes apply?) Their salaries at these companies start at about £15,000 per year. Average salaries are about £20,000 for all tax consultants. Those operating from accountancy firms can make as much as £80,000 per year.

STOCKBROKER

Trades securities for his clients and collects a percentage fee on each transaction. Brokers also give their clients investment advice. A broker's income depends on how much business he does; a declining market can actually benefit brokers if it causes more stocks to be traded. City brokers in big firms average about £40,000 per year. Those in smaller firms, considerably less.

STOCKJOBBER

Jobbers do the actual dealing in securities on the London Stock Exchange. The margin between the price they pay for securities and the price at which they sell them represents their profit margin — their income. Jobbers trade securities for brokers with whom they negotiate to determine the price that applies to clients. A jobber's income will vary with his trading skill and with the number of trades that he makes. An average jobber might earn £25,000 per year. The best-paid jobber last year earned £80,000 while the Directors of his stockjobbing company earned just under £100,000 per year.

AUTHORISED CLERK
This position is essentially an assistant jobber. The authorised clerk can buy and sell securities on the exchange under the direction of a jobber. Clerks earnings can vary with jobbers, but an average figure would be around £12,000 per year.

INVESTMENT ADVISOR
These advisors study clients' assets and financial needs and manage their funds accordingly. The investment advisor is not a broker, however. Perhaps the essential difference betwen the advice a broker gives and that offered by an investment advisor is that the advisor works for a very few clients — often only one — and advises them about other assets in addition to securities. Advisors sometimes work on commission, but those on salaries (employed by banks, for example) will average £20,000 per year.

INVESTMENT ANALYST
An investment analyst is usually an expert on one particular industry. They will be called in to offer advice as to whether a particular investment in that industry will be profitable. Analysts are employed by brokerage firms and especially by banks. A great number are paid by the job, but those on salaries earn about £17,000.

RECEIVERSHIP/INSOLVENCY EXPERTS

Usually accountants or solicitors, these experts specialise in the financial problems of bank-ruptcy, offering advice both on the best way of filing for receivership and on collecting debts from such companies. The positions are usually attached to accountancy firms, management consultancies, or merchant banks. The job requires prior experience in business as a pre-requisite to entry. Salaries begin at about £15,000 per year and, if successful, an employee would be likely to move on to a different position within the firm. The result is that salaries for insolvency jobs rarely go much higher.

INTERNATIONAL TRADERS

Employees in these positions are involved in negotiating large purchases or sales betweeen companies in different countries. These jobs differ from buyers and sales representatives in that the deals are much larger (frequently millions of pounds) and the traders must be bilingual. Salaries usually start at £10,000 per year, but the jobs requires previous business experience.

PENSION FUND MANAGERS

This job requires a background in accountancy or in investment planning. Most companies have their own pension programmes, but usually turn to outside consultants to manage them. The job of the pension fund manager is to guard the fund's solvency and make certain that expected income matches expected payments. Some actuarial work may be involved, too. Pension fund managers are well-paid — between £25,000 and £30,000 per year. In recent years they have become the largest influences on the Stock Exchange and property worlds. Their salaries reflect both this power and their large responsibility.

INSURANCE

The insurance industry is one of the healthiest in Britain. Overseas demand, particularly for maritime insurance, has kept the market expanding and the number of jobs increasing. Many of these jobs are highly technical and unique to the insurance business (such as those requiring actuarial skills).

	£ per year
Trainees 'A' Level	3,500
Trainees Graduates	3,700
Assistant Underwriters	5,600
Senior Underwriters	11,500
Technicians	5,400
Placing Brokers	9,700
Claims Brokers	7,000 - 8,500
Account Handlers	8,200 - 9,300
Pension Administrators	7,500

Perks: Insurance is usually provided by the company.

ECONOMISTS

The market for economists is perhaps the only job market that seems to improve during a recession (like that for doctors during a plague). The title is generally taken to refer to those who study economy-wide forces and predict their influences on subsections of the economy. Economists with an honours degree usually begin work at £7,000 per year. Those with graduate degrees would start at about £8,000 per year. The enthusiasm for economists in business (such as it is) is a relatively new phenomenon; as a result, it is difficult to estimate career earnings because most corporate economists are in the early stages of their careers. Those in their early thirties, however, earn an average of about £15,500 per year. Academic economists are paid on the standard University Lecturer-Professor scale.

ACCOUNTANCY

Like the Law, Accountancy is a profession divided between private firms and commercial or industrial employers. Responsibilities and practices can be quite different in the two – as can salaries – which is why separate schedules for each are listed below. Almost all Chartered Accountants are university graduates, and this is likely to be even more frequently the case in the future. It is still possible, though, to become a contracted student in a firm and to be trained by them. Schedules for these positions are also listed below. These salaries are for the London area. Salaries here are about 20 per cent higher than in the rest of the U.K.; the greatest difference tends to be in starting salaries.

In Firms	£ per year
Students entering four year training contracts	3,500
University graduates entering three year contracts	4,200
Chartered Accountants (newly qualified)	8,000 – 9,500
Chartered Accountants (Audit Managers – middle level)	11,000 – 12,500
Salaried Partners	16,000 – 18,000

The larger, well-known accountancy firms in the City are a world unto themselves – as are their salaries. University graduates entering contracts earn as much as £6,000 per year. Middle level managers would average about £16,000. Senior partners can earn over £100,000 – earnings over £200,000 have been reported.

In Industry or Commerce	£ per year
Students entering four year training contracts	4,000
University graduates entering three year contracts	4,500
Qualified Accountants	8,500 – 12,000
Chief Accountants	13,000 – 15,000
Finance Directors	17,000 – 19,000

Finance Directors in the largest companies average aboiut £30,000 per year.

Uncertified Assistants
  (bookkeepers, clerks, etc.)   3,500 – 4,500
More senior uncertified positions 6,500 – 8,500

Perks: Partners actually own the firm and have great discretion in setting their hours and perks. They can also take profits in lieu of salary.

VALUER
A valuer assesses the value of property – both residential and commercial – to determine an accurate price or to establish taxation or insurance rates. Valuers in the Civil Service earn between £8,500 and £12,500 per year – rising to £20,500 with administrative responsibilities. Those in the private sector are usually paid a commission or flat rate per job. Annual earnings vary with the quantity and type of work undertaken.

ESTATE AGENTS
Estate agents trade and manage property on behalf of clients, charging a commission on the transactions. This is usually one and a half per cent.

MANAGEMENT CONSULTANTS

Provide expert advice and objective opinions on management problems. Consultants come from academic as well as business communities, and the fees are often negotiated in a very casual way. They are always high. University members usually work for about £100 per day, sometimes consider-ably more. Professional consulting groups – often the consulting division of large accounting firms and merchant banks – charge by the hour or by the day. The hourly charge would vary from £20 for work performed by the most junior consultants to £200 for the most senior. The average daily charge is about £400. Earnings for those working independently will depend entirely on how much work they do. Those employed by firms will enter those company and plant level agreements are. Officers in the employer assoc-iations will be well paid, however, averaging about £25,000 per year for the top jobs and £15,000 for assistants from university at a salary of about £8,000 per year – slightly more for those with an advanced technical degree. Earnings can rise to upwards of £80,000 per year. Many young consultants leave their firms after a few years having, found (or perhaps created) desirable management positions in companies.

INDUSTRIAL RELATIONS OFFICERS/SPECIALISTS

Where the workers in a company are represented by a trade union, many of the usual functions of the personnel department must be negotiated with the unions (notably the wage and salary structure). The job of the Industrial Relations Officer is to represent the company in those negotiations. Not all of these jobs are with companies, however. Most are with employer associations who conduct negotiations on behalf of their constituent members. Some of these member companies might retain industrial relations experts to negotiate supplementary agreements at the plant or company level. Their pay would be slightly less than for personnel officers, depending on how important those company and plant level agreements are. Officers in the employers associations will be well paid, however, averaging about £25,000 per year for the top jobs and £15,000 for assistants.

TEACHERS
Primary, Secondary, and Further Education
Colleges

The determination of pay for teachers received considerable attention this year when it was turned over to the Clegg Commission on Pay Comparability. Negotiations between teachers and management take place in Burnham Committees composed of representatives from each side. The Houghton Committee investigated the problem and proposed a set of principles to govern teachers' pay — based mainly on comparisons with jobs elsewhere. In 1980, the Clegg Commission took over and recommended increases based on the earnings of similar graduates who entered different occupations. These are reproduced below. Increases in grade correspond to the age of the class being taught. A new settlement just reached is expected to add about 7 per cent to these figures for 1981.

Schools	£ per year
Qualified Teacher Scale 1	3,780 − 5,946
Good Honours Graduate	6,393
Senior Teacher	6,888 − 9,267
Deputy Head Teacher	4,728 − 11,544
Head Teacher	6,651 − 15,732

Colleges	£ per year
Lecturer I	4,071 – 6,801
Lecturer II	5,229 – 8,436
Senior Lecturer	7,785 – 9,822
Principal Lecturer	9,138 – 11,568
Head of Department	7,593 – 13,479
Vice-Principal	8,514 – 17,766
Principal	9,996 – 21,243

UNIVERSITY TEACHERS
Lecturers/Readers/ Professors

University resources have been reduced substantially in the past two years, and some departments are being phased-out as student numbers decline. While very few permanent jobs are being advertised, the number of part-time and temporary positions has actually increased – no doubt as a less expensive way of meeting teaching requirements. The following rates are minimums which in many cases are supplemented through additional payments as well as 'in kind' benefits. Pay increases within each category with age. The Association of University Teachers is currently involved in negotiations with the government which should raise these rates by 6-13 per cent (the government's and Association's offers, respectively).

	£ per year
Lecturer	5,505 – 11,575
Reader	11,165 – 13,980
Professor (minimum)	14,275
(average)	16,765

Perks: Some Oxford and Cambridge colleges and centres will pay salaries as much as £2,000 in addition to these rates. Most provide allowances

for housing — sometimes over £2,000 — as well as
for other expenses. In addition, Fellows receive
free meals in College and use of College
facilities. Some departments provide an added
inducement by freeing Fellows from teaching
obligations in order that they may devote
themselves full time to research. University
teachers receive about one term of paid leave for
every six in residence.

Arrangements at some colleges allow Fellows to
live outside the university. At All Souls for
example many Fellows have appointments in other
universities or in wholly different professions.

ENGINEERS

The resurgence of interest in high technology has
focused attention on the engineering profession
and its role in industrial progress and
innovation. Engineers are at work in every
industry; almost one-third are involved in some
sort of management. It is difficult, therefore,
to say much about engineers as a group. But one
can identify two categories of workers throughout the economy. Technical engineers are involved
with more practical considerations, while
Chartered Engineers are more likely to handle
design and planning work, the latter having
greater skills.

	£ per year
All Technical Engineers	7,200
All Chartered Engineers	8,650

Chartered Engineers by educational background:

	£ per year
Non-graduates	9,000
Graduates	8,200
Post-graduates	9,400

The surprising fact that median earnings for graduates are lower than for non-graduates may be due to the age distribution in each group. Graduates earn more than non-graduates of the same age, but the former may on average be a younger group.

Additional compensation is provided for work that may be dangerous and for jobs that may require travel. The compensation for travel increases with the employer's age. It has been calculated that engineers in education earn about £5,000 less than similarly qualified engineers elsewhere.

MEDIAN EARNINGS BY INDUSTRY

	Technical Engineers £ per year	Chartered Engineers £ per year
Chemical	8,400	9,600
Petroleum	9,000	10,950
Metal Manufacture	7,320	8,450
Machine Tools	7,008	7,680
Industrial Plant	7,800	8,040
Electrical machinery	6,960	8,100
Electronic	6,750	7,680
Shipbuilding and marine	7,230	9,530
Aircraft or aero engine	6,480	7,950
Vehicle Manufacture	6,830	7,800
Mining	9,500	10,250
Agriculture	6,350	7,800
Construction	6,500	8,250
Consulting	7,200	8,400
Computer technology	8,200	8,890
Gas	7,450	9,000
Electricity generation	8,650	9,840
Water	6,800	8,160
Transport	7,530	8,400
Docks and harbours	-	9,120

	Technical Engineers £ per year	Chartered Engineers £ per year
Postal and telecommunications	8,050	9,360
Central government	6,890	10,000
Local Government	6,480	8,550
Research	6,680	8,650
University	6,720	9,530
Technical college	7,320	8,650
School	6,060	6,250
The Armed Forces	6,970	8,820

MEDIAN EARNINGS BY FIELD

Engineers by Professional Group	£ per year
Royal Aereonautical Society	8,810
Institution of Chemical Engineers	9,330
Institution of Civil Engineers	8,150
Institution of Electrical Engineers	8,520
Institution of Electronic and Radio Engineers	8,500
Institute of Energy	8,890
Institution of Gas Engineers	9,420
Institute of Marine Engineers	9,600
Institution of Mechanical Engineers	8,900
Institution of Metallurgists	7,830
Institution of Mining and Metallurgy	10,075

	£ per year
Institution of Mining Engineers	10,250
Institution of Municipal Engineers	8,500
Royal Institution of Naval Architects	9,840
Institution of Production Engineers	8,350
Institution of Structural Engineers	8,450
All Chartered Engineers	8,650

The Following Table Shows What Percentage of Engineers Work in Which Field

1.8%	Self Employed
45.6%	Industrial/Commerical Company
8.9%	Firm of Consultants
3.3%	Public Corporation
14.1%	Nationalised Industry
2.8%	Regional Authority
11.2%	Local Authority
5.5%	Central Government
1.5%	Armed Forces
2.5%	University
2.8%	Other Employer

CHAPTER FOUR

Writers, Artists, Entertainers and Sportsmen

ARTISTS

Most artists could be classified as entrepreneurs in that they organise and produce their own products and receive income based on the receipts. It is impossible, therefore, to estimate accurately how much various types of artist would earn. It is possible to describe the way in which they sell their work - which, in turn, determines their income. A given painting or piece first requires an initial outlay for materials, often an expensive outlay, which is borne by the artist. It is a consideration, therefore, in setting the price of the painting. Other important factors include the amount of work that went into producing it as well as the subjective estimate of its quality by the artist. The most important factor, however, is how much the artist thinks the market will bear, and that depends largely on where it is sold. Galleries sell works for artists and charge a commission that is based on the clientele they attract. Well established galleries in London can charge commissions of 50 - 60 per cent. A common figure in regional centres might be closer to 20 per cent. After the commissions and the cost of materials are deducted, it is possible for an unestablished artist to lose money on a piece, intentionally setting the price low in order to get some work sold. There are artists who take on a contract or commission to produce a given painting for a given customer - portrait painters, for example. A good one can earn £1,000 - 2,000 per portrait.

The highest price paid for a painting by a living United Kingdom artist is £89,890. The painting, by Francis Bacon, was however bought at auction and not directly from the artist.

MUSICIANS

The rates of pay for musicians form an extremely complicated schedule, varying according to the nature of performances, as well as their location. Many of the arrangements determining pay are negotiated at the 'job. They may range far above the basic union rates and may include a variety of supplemental payments for transport, equipment portage, subsistence and late performances. Rates for soloists and for featured groups are negotiated on behalf of the performers by agents who also settle the specific terms of the show. The following figures are basic rates for musicians performing in groups and accompanying performances.

Variety Shows/Stage Bands - £30 performing in an orchestra pit, £31.80 on stage for a three-hour performance plus one rehearsal. Overtime is paid at a rate of £3.60 for each quarter hour.

Night Club/Cabaret - £110 per week for six one-and-a-half hour performances spread over six days, including rehearsals.

Cinema Work — £40 for three-hour sessions; T.V. filmwork pays £70 for 4-hour sessions. Commercial T.V. work pays £36 for three-hour sessions with supplements worth about £25.

Rehearsal Pianists earn £13.20 per two-hour session; £132 for a thirty-hour session spread over 5 days.

The range of possible performances and their circumstances are infinite. In part, that explains why informal, ad hoc arrangements over pay are necessary. Musicians are rarely guaranteed employment and rely on informal networks of contacts in order to locate work.

It is reported that Paul McCartney earned in excess of £25,000,000 in 1980, but the vast majority of this must have come from royalty payments.

THEATRE

As is the practice in the entertainment industry, performers on the stage negotiate individual contracts with their employers. But Actor's Equity has established minimum weekly rates which are printed below. Of course, thespians get paid only as long as their shows run — which could be considerably less than a full working year. Salaries can range quite high above these minimums, but the average should be similar.

	£ per week
Children	45.00
Actors/Actresses (in provinces)	78.00
(in London)	95.00

Perks: Subsistence allowance of £17.40 per week when playing in the provinces. An allowance of £29.00 is paid to those on tour.

Theatre Administration (provincial)	£ per week
Ushers	20.00
Box Office Staff	45.00
Box Office Managers	77.00
Directors	100.00
Deputy Stage Manager	97.50
Stage Manager	109.20

Salaries in the West End of London are one-third higher. In addition to his salary, the Director receives a minimum allowance of £100 per show to cover expenses.

Perks: The roar of the crowd.

MAKE-UP ARTIST

Apply cosmetics to enhance appearances or to create special effects. Make-up Artists in television earn between £6,000 and £7,400 per year, while those in the theatre earn slightly less - £5,500 to £6,500 on average. Make-up Artists who work in film can earn considerably more, particularly for special effects which are often subcontracted to independent companies. Artists in this end of the business are paid by the job, but their annual earnings can exceed £8,000 - 9,000 per year.

DANCERS

Dancers pay can vary a great deal depending on the discretion of their producers and the size of the production budget. And, of course, established dancers with a large following negotiate individual contracts. Those working in shows receive £100 - £120 per week in the West End; about £80 per week when working in the provinces plus expenses for a minimum of eight weeks accommodation, even if the show does not run that long. Those touring as members of a featured group earn about £200 per week. As with other performers, however, dancers are only paid when their shows are running, and that may not be all that often.

CIRCUS PERFORMERS

The organisation of a circus might be described as a collection of independent entrepreneurs who provide their own props and sign individual contracts with the owner – the Circus Director. The artists and their families do take part in the general production, though, selling programmes and taking tickets. They sign seasonal contracts and are paid by the week for a fixed number of performances, usually around five per week. Fees vary not only with how professional and famous the act is but also with the degree of risk involved. Not all acts that appear risky actually are, however. For example, lion-tamers frequently just present animals that have been trained by someone else. Britain pays performers remarkably low fees by comparison with other countries. It is not uncommon to earn 10 times as much performing in the Middle East or in the U.S.A. When the circus travels abroad, the Director pays travel and maintenance costs for the performers. This is one industry where women tend to be paid more than men; their glamour is a box office draw. The figure below represents a range of earnings for average performers.

	£ per week
Box office staff	20 – 50
Box Officer Managers	80 – 90
Jugglers, clowns, gymnasts	50 – 1000
Ringmaster	175 – 200
Trapese artists and lion tamers	200 – 300

Perks: Meet interesting people.
Hours are short but rehearsals may be time consuming.

PHOTOGRAPHERS

While all photographers take pictures, the type of pictures that they take determines not only their salaries but also their terms of employment. A number of photographers go out on location to photograph weddings and advertising displays. These tend to be self-employed, owning their own equipment and either charging set fees or taking commissions on reproductions. Other photographers, however, work in industry or for large studios. They do not usually own the equipment and are paid a salary for a normal working week. These salaries are set out below. Independent and freelance photographers have responsibilities that correspond to the last three or four grades, but obviously the variance in their earnings would be very great, corresponding to the quality of their work and the number of jobs they do.

	£ per year
Laboratory Assistants (essentially trainees)	1,500 – 2,400
Assistant Technicians (basic darkroom work)	2,400 – 3,000
Junior Photographers (some processing)	3,000 – 4,300
Photographers (works with clients)	4,400 – 6,500
Senior Photographers (specialised techniques)	7,300 – 9,000
Principal Photographer and Department Manager	8,300 – 9,000

High Street photographers are independent businessmen paid by the job. Their earnings depend not just on the quantity of work they undertake, but also on the type of work.

Advertising and commercial work is the best paid - a small one-off shot might pay £25 while rates for a full day's shooting average about £200. The photographers pays his expenses from these fees. Portraiture pays from £25 for very basic prints to £150 or more for enlarged framed prints. Work due for magazines is sometimes paid by comission based on the publication's sales. A small print used in a national magazine, for example, might earn the photographer about £50.

The top photographers work through agents who negotiate for each assignment. Lord Snowdon charges approximately £1,000 per day with assistants' and film and processing on top. David Bailey appears to be slightly cheaper at £800 - £1,000 per day but no extra for assistant. You will however have to pay for his film and processing.

TELEVISION

The television industry is divided into two parts: public and private. The public sector - British Broadcasting Corporation - does a great deal of its own programming and trains its own staff. The private sector, Independent Television, buys much of its programming from the United States and rarely trains its own staff. The conditions in the private sector are worse. Manning levels are lower and fewer resources may be available, but the pay is between 40 and 60 per cent higher. The following jobs and salaries are for the BBC.

Technical Staff	£ per year	
	Regions	London
Cameramen	7,837	8,562
Assistant Cameramen	6,568	7,298
Sound Recordists	7,172	7,902
Film Editor	7,172	7,902
Assistant Film Editor	5,833	6,613

The technical staff work many overtime hours which are not accounted for in the figures above. Employees working on certain, large front line programmes such as Panorama or Nationwide are paid premium rates. Film editors on these shows earn £8,619 per year while assistants earn £7,200.

Editorial Staff	£ per week — London
Researcher	6 - 7,500
Assistant Producer	7,500 - 9,000
Producer	8,500 - 12,000
Senior Producer	11 - 14,000
Reporters	14 - 20,000
Editors	15 - 20,000

Reporters are well-paid, but their tenure is uncertain as most work on two-year contracts.

Senior Staff

	£ per year
Heads of Departments e.g. News or Current Affairs)	20-28,000
Controllers (e.g. BBC 1 and 2)	29-35,000

Both the B.B.C. and the I.B.A. are controlled by boards of governors. Mr. George Howard, chairman of the B.B.C. is paid £15,000 while Lady Plowden who does the equivalent job for the I.B.A. receives £19,048. The Vice Chairman, The Hon.Mark Bonham Carter and Lord Thompson of Monifieth were paid £3,600 and £5,000 respectively by the B.B.C. and I.B.A. Governors at the B.B.C. are paid between £1,800 and £3,600 while all members of the I.B.A. earn £2,500. The highest paid member of the staff of the B.B.C. earns £35,000 - 40,000 according to the statement of accounts for 1980. Sir Ian Trethowan is the Director General.

CINEMA WORKERS

There are about five hundred cinemas in Britain, each graded according to their size. They employ a large number of part-timers who work between 15 and 30 hours per week – coinciding with performance times. The workforce tends to be disproportionately young and female. The following are weekly minimum rates for cinema jobs. Because the performances are on a regular schedule, overtime work is less important than in other jobs. Actual earnings will be about 15 – 20 per cent above these rates. Part-time workers are paid on an hourly basis.

	£ per week
Projectionists	51.50 – 59.00
Head attendants	46.45 – 48.05
Attendants	46.45 – 47.55
Cashiers clerks	48.40 – 49.00
Cashiers	47.40 – 48.50

Sunday workers and night workers (after the last performance) are paid at premium rates. Perks: get to see 'Gone with the Wind' four times every day for a week.

RADIO STAFF

Production and technical staff negotiate together with the Independent Radio Contractors to set salaries in private sector broadcasting. These salaries are higher than in the BBC but conditions tend to be less salubrious.

	£ per year
Junior production	2,784
and junior technicians	3,161 after 4 years
Presenters, Researchers	3,505
Sound engineers	4,300 after 6 years

	£ per year
Senior presenters and engineers	5,290
After 6 years	6,480
Senior engineers and producers	5,990
After 6 years	7,210

Hours: Rotating pattern of shifts which may include weekend and night work. There is a 12% allowance for work between 2.00 and 5.00 a.m.

JOURNALISTS
Collect and report on news items, sometimes providing commentary as well.

Salaries for Provincial Journalists
By Geographic Area

	£ per week
Where no other newspapers are published	92.50–102.50
Areas between 12 and 30 miles from Charing Cross	93.50–103.50
Areas within 12 miles of Charing Cross where newspaper's circulation is under 30,000	94.50–104.50
Daily newspapers with circulation between 30,000 and 150,000	98.50–110.50
Local printed weekly for London area	101.80–111.80
Local papers printed daily for London area	104.80–119.80
London Office of Provincial Daily Paper	108.50–128.50

Indentured trainees earn approximately £60 per week regardless of geographic area.

Provincial journalists work 78 hours every two weeks. By the end of 1981, hours are scheduled to fall to 75 for the same period.

Salaries for Fleet Street newspapers are negotiated separately at each paper. Salaries at the Tabloid papers (e.g. Sun and Daily Mirror) tend to be the highest – starting at about £13,000 per year versus £10,500 at The Times. Average salaries at the major papers (e.g. Financial Times, Guardian, Times) would be between £13,000 – 14,000.

It is important to note that the lowest-level starting positions at these papers are usually filled by journalists with considerable experience. The traditional career path is for journalists to enter Fleet Street jobs after three or more years working on provincial papers. This connection, while still strong, has been eroded somewhat in recent years.

Journalists in Commercial Radio

	£ per year
Copy Writers, voice reporting and interviewing	5,200–6,200
Senior Writers	5,970–7,800
Head of News Section	7,070–8,870

Hours will be reduced to 35 in 1981. An allowance of £4 a week is paid to offset the costs of essential publications.

BOOK PUBLISHING

Book publishing is still considered a desirable
profession for young graduates although it does
not have quite the same glamour as Fleet Street
or television. Most entrants into editorial and
marketing jobs have degrees. Some firms are very
small with fewer than five members of staff,
while the biggest employ about 500. Most of the
larger firms are unionised to some extent. The
Association of Scientific, Technical and
Managerial Staff and the National Union of
Journalists have the strongest representation.
negotiations are always at the individual company
level. Salary scales for a typical large firm are
given below.

	£ per year
Senior Commissioning Editor with managerial responsibilities	9 – 15,000
Senior Commissioning Editors (finding authors)	8 – 11,000
Commissioning Editors	7 – 10,000
Assistant Editors (editing typescripts)	5 – 8,000
Editorial Assistants	4 – 6,000
Marketing/Sales Managers	8 – 11,000
Advertising Managers	7 – 10,000
Marketing/Publicity Controllers	5 – 8,000
Marketing/Publicity Assistants	4 – 6,000
Senior Sales Reps	6 – 9,000
Production/Design Managers	8 – 11,000
Senior Production/ Design Controllers	6 – 9,000
Production Controllers/ Designers	5 – 8,000

	£ per year
Production Assistants	5 - 7,000
Distribution Managers	9 - 17,000
Stock Managers	8 - 11,000
Transport Managers	7 - 10,000

Freelance copy editing and indexing and proof reading £3.00 - £3.50 per hour. Sales representatives on commission take 5 to 10 per cent of what the bookseller pays the publisher.

LIBRARIANS
Plan future acquisitions and index and present current ones. Academic librarians are paid according to university scales. Business librarians can earn as much as £17,000 per year when their speciality is in demand.

INDUSTRIAL DESIGNERS/ARTISTS
Create designs for products, combining its function in an aesthetic form. They consider costs and performance requirements in the development of their designs. Industrial designers also work with architects and advertising consultants in the development of displays, illustrations and in the construction of similations and models. The work varies a great deal between industries; the job of an industrial artist working for a magazine is quite different from that of an industrial designer in shipbuilding. The following list represents pay scales for industrial designers in different industries.

In the Civil Service, for everything from research councils to the National Portrait Gallery, the job title is Graphic Artist, and most of the work consists of developing displays and models rather than products.

	£ per year
Graphic Officer (basic grade)	4,700 – 5,300
(Highest grade)	7,300 – 8,600

The London allowance is £780 per year for inner and £325 per year for outer London.

British Broadcasting Corporation – employs a range of industrial designers/artists who design sets and produce illustrations for television.

	£ per year
Design Assistant (basic grade)	4,800 – 5,950
Designer	8,250 – 10,500
Design Manager (highest grade)	11,875 – 15,650

The London allowance is £730 per year.

Engineering – employs industrial designers as technical illustrators and product designers.

	£ per year
Technical Illustrator	5,400
Technical Artist	5,900
Model Maker	5,850
Stylist	6,100

Publishing – industrial artists work almost entirely as illustrators.

	£ per year
Basic Grade	4,500
Highest Grade	10,000

Publishing also employs a large number of free-lance illustrators who sometimes receive a royalty on the proceeds of published material.

Furniture design – essentially product designers.

	£ per year
Basic Grade	4,000
Average earnings	8,000

Some furniture designers receive a commission on their work. Those whose products are in demand can earn considerably more through comissions – £10,000 – £12,000 per year.

DRAUGHTSMEN

	£ per year
Tracers	4,400 – 4,900
Drawing office assistants	4,500 – 5,200
Standard engineers	5,300 – 6,000
Draughtsmen	5,500 – 6,200
Draughtsmen/designers	5,800 – 6,500
Drawing office manager	6,500 – 7,500

FOOTBALLERS

There is tremendous variance in the earnings of football players. The minimum wage for a player under full contract is £30 per week over an entire year. Average earnings are considerably higher:

	£ per year
Fourth Division	5,000
Third Division	6,000
Second Division	9,000
First Division	11,000

An extremely well-paid side, such as Liverpool First Division, will have average earnings of about £16,000 per year. Members of First Teams are typically on bonus systems which can run as high as £500 per point. The best-paid players

will earn about £35,000 this year; best-paid
managers about the same. Winning players on a cup
final team can earn about £10,000 each from that
one game. Players also receive 10 per cent of
their transfer fees.

RUGBY FOOTBALLERS

The game of Rugby is divided into two groups
Rugby Union where the players receive compensation only for expenses and Rugby League where
players are paid. There is some debate as to
whether the differences in the status of the
players in Union and League is really as simple
as amateur or professional.

League players are paid by the game - an average
of £75 for a home win, slightly more for a win
away from home, and an average of £40 for
losses. An interesting aspect of League pay
scales is that there is almost no difference in
cash earnings betwen players on the same team. In
additon to payments by game, players also receive
a fee for 'signing on' with a team - average
around £500, but can rise as high as £20,000. A
League player earning £5,000 per year would be
considered quite well-paid, but remember that
players only get paid if they play. They are not
on salaries.

CRICKETERS

County cricket players are usually paid a base
salary and participate in a system of bonus
payments that bring average earnings to around
£4,000 per year. Test-match players are reported
to earn around £1,000 per match after bonuses,
etc. A player's main source of income, however,
comes from his 'benefit year' when his team
organises a series of events to raise money on
his behalf (lotteries, special matches, etc.) The

earnings from a benefit year frequently exceed
£30,000.

Football, rugby and cricket now benefit from
endorsements and special arrangements with
sponsors which add to player's earnings.

HORSE RACING
In this sport, an industry in itself, it is
difficult to assess earnings. Averages are misleading since the very few earn a great deal and
the majority are paid very low wages for long
and unsocial hours.

Jockeys
A professional jockey will earn about £36 for
each race and receive 10 per cent of the prize
money. It should be borne in mind that he will
often have four rides in a single day and that
racing has a six-day week. Willie Carson was
champion jockey in 1980 with 165 wins, but Lester
Piggot won a place in nearly a quarter of all his
races. The percentage of winnings is obviously
therefore a highly significant factor when
assessing a jockey's income.

Stable Lads
These men and women, who can be of any age, are
responsible for the hard work around the
trainers' stables. They also exercise the horses
and receive a minimum wage of £53 per forty-hour
week, but their hours are, by comparison with
other industries, unsociable in the extreme.

Owners
It is almost impossible to draw any conclusions
about owners as a group, although it has been
reported that the average horse on the flat earns
about £2,000 and costs about £6,000 in any one

year. Of all the parts of the industry owners'earnings are the biggest nonsense when averaged. In 1980 Lord Weinstock's family owned Ela-Mana-Mou which won four races and earned £236,332. The horse cost half a million pounds in 1979. On the other hand Henbit, which won the Derby and with it a prize of £166,820, cost only £12,000. It is however in stud fees that these horses really generate a profit for their owners as well as with the bookmaker (if the owner is so inclined).

CHAPTER FIVE

Hotel, Catering and Domestic Trades

CATERING

The catering industry includes all restaurants, hotels, and private catering operations. In its structure, catering is almost two separate industries: one massive and sophisticated, dominated by conglomerates and the other small, family operations. Business is very competitive and wages are low – not much above the levels set for catering by the relevant Wages Councils. Immigrants make up a large proportion of the labour force.

	£ per week
Licensed Non-Residential Establishments	57.00

Perks: Meals are provided for 35p each; living in arrangements for £7 per week.
The London allowance is £5 per week.

Unlicensed Non-Residential Establishments

	£ per week
Waiting staff	51.00
Cashiers and service cooks	52.00

	£ per week
Floor supervisors	53.00
Cooks and assistant managers	55.00
Head cooks or chefs	57.00

Perks: Meals are free. Waiting staff get tips. London allowance is £2 per week. Working week is 36 hours.

Licensed Restaurants and Residential Establishments

	£ per week
Waiters and waitresses	49.00
Other workers	57.60
Chefs	120-130

Perks: Service workers get tips — sometimes shared with other workers and with the chef. London Allowance £4.00.

Better Restaurants in London	£ per week
Waiting Staff	67.50
Headwaiters	70.00

	£ per year
Commis (Training) Chef	3,500 — 4,000
Sous (2nd) Chef	7,500
Head Chef	10,000 — 20,000

Perks: Tips can be quite large — £20-£30 per server per shift is not uncommon, but they are usually split several ways.

HOTELS

The following jobs are those common to most hotels, although some of these jobs might not exist in the smaller ones. In addition, the large hotels are frequently in metropolitan areas where the general wage level is higher.

	£ per year	
	Manager	Assistant Manager
Hotel Groups	12-15,000	8 - 10,000
Large Hotels	10-11,000	6 - 7,000
Medium-sized hotels	8,500	4 - 5,400
Small Hotels	6,500	3 - 5,400

Head Receptionists, Head Housekeepers

Earn from £3,500 per year in small hotels to £6,000 in hotel groups. Receptionists and telephonists in most hotels earn about £70 per week. Hours can be quite irregular and may include substantial overtime work.

Hall Porters

Earn about £70 per week in the big hotels; closer to £60 in smaller ones. They can earn tips, however.

Bar Staff

Earn slightly more than porters - £80 per week in the larger hotels.

Chambermaids

Are paid close to £65 per week when they work a 40-hour week. It is worth pointing out that this is often not the case. If paid by the hour, they earn about £1.75.

In many cases, accommodation is provided by the hotel for its staff - who may choose whether or not to take it. If they do, however, a deduction is made from their salary. Hotels gain certain advantages from having live-in employees; for example, it is easy to find them for overtime and odd shift work.

DOORMEN

Restrict access to those with legitimate interests there; also known for holding doors

open when one passes through them. Doormen often
are required to wear uniforms which are usually
provided by the employer. Much of the work is
done in the evening, although premium rates for
unsocial hours are rare. Basic rates for doormen
average between £50 and £60 per week, but
earnings vary far more. Tips can substantially
increase one's earnings at the more expensive
restaurants and hotels: sometimes £10 - 15 per
night. Tips vary with services performed - such
as hailing cabs and providing directions.
Earnings for these jobs average between £80 - £90
per week. Earnings for jobs at less salubrious
spots - where the doorman might also be responsible for removing undesirables - would be closer
to £70. Doormen usually work six-day shifts, but
weekly hours average about 40.

OFF-LICENCE STAFF
These workers are usually employees of large
companies who set the rates of pay for management according to the size of the shop. Bonuses
can add substantially to their earnings.

	£ per year
Managers - largest shops	6,700 - 7,500
- smallest shops	4,500 - 5,000

	£ per week
Senior Staff	70.00
Cellar Labourers	60.00

SCHOOL MEALS PERSONNEL

	£ per week
Principal (administration, budgets, etc.)	9,100
Senior Organiser (staff manager)	6,900

	£ per week
Organiser (oversees serving, etc.)	6,500
Assistants	3,500–5,000

COLLEGE/UNIVERSITY MANUAL STAFF

The following positions are those associated with the domestic side of college life. The earnings associated with each position are for full-time work. Many employees work only part time and will therefore earn considerably less.

	£ Per Week
Head Chef/Supervisor	105.00
Second Chef/Cooks	90.00
Kitchen Hand	70.00
Serving Staff (almost all part-time)	1.00 per hour
Head Gardeners	80.00
Groundsmen	70.00
Head Porters	80.00
Porters (almost all part-time)	1.20 per hour
Security Staff	75.00
Cleaners (almost all part-time)	1.20 per hour

Oxbridge colleges provide better perks than elsewhere, but earnings there are considerably lower. Many colleges pay all but the supervisory staff £1.40 per hour, and because the work is often less than 40 hours per week, total earnings are low. The benefits, though, include free or subsidised housing, as well as free meals for those living in college. Benefits outside Oxbridge are very similar to those for service workers in the rest of the economy, but most university manual workers receive 33 days of holiday per year.

CLEANERS

Cleaning is a big business, dominated in urban areas by large contractors. The Low Pay Unit estimates that 100,000 cleaners currently work for contractors in this highly competitive industry. The government is the single largest consumer of cleaning services, although since the 1960s, it has shifted from a policy of employing cleaners to contracting the work out to the private sector. Almost all cleaners are women, most working only part-time. Trade union representation and membership is low. Cleaning is one of the worst-paid jobs in Britain. There is no Wages Council order for this industry.

	£ per week
Cleaners employed by contractors	73.00 (in London)
Chambermaids	60.00
College cleaners and those employed permanently on a site	1.50 per hour

Wages can, of course, be higher. These figures represent an average. However, because cleaning cannot be done during business hours, cleaners must work what are usually thought to be unsocial hours (after 6.00 p.m.). There is no shift pay for this work. Cleaners in manufacturing, whose earnings are tied to the plant pay structure, would earn substantially more – over £90 per week in engineering.

Perks: Chambermaids often receive accommodation as part of their earnings, although deductions for housing are quite common. College cleaners are sometimes provided with housing; if the housing is in college, meals are often included. College cleaners – like chambermaids – sometimes receive tips which might average £100 per year.

HOUSEKEEPERS

Combine the services of cook, cleaner, butler and sometimes seamstress, too. Housekeepers — as opposed to maids or cooks — almost always live on the premises, receiving their meals and lodgings free. Earnings are quite low — about £35 per week — and conditions vary tremendously between employers. The employment relationship tends towards paternalism, and it is not uncommon for the housekeeper to stay on until they (or the employer) dies. Vacations tend to be short, if at all, and days off are usually limited to an afternoon or so per week. Bonuses tend to be in the form of presents.

HOME ECONOMISTS

Are experts in domestic science — running the affairs of a household in an efficient and effective manner. They are employed to teach in schools and by the food industry to develop and test recipes, design displays and give demonstrations. Pay averages about £6 - 7,000 per year.

CHAPTER SIX

Office, Clerical and Allied Jobs

DIRECTORS

Directors form the general policies to be pursued by a company. They are also known as Board Members — from the Board of Directors. Executive Directors have management responsibilities within the company — director of production, for example, and heads of departments are usually given executive directorships in order that they can supply the rest of the board with accurate information about the company's position. Non-executive directors come from outside the company. They are usually experts on a particular aspect of business or politics, and their information and contacts are sought to aid the board in constructing accurate and reasonable long-term plans. The selection and membership of the non-executive directors has been of considerable interest to students of corporations who sometimes argue, for example, that they are chosen from the boards of other companies in order to provide links between boards. These links give companies inside information on competitors, government plans, and in so doing allow the board to plan more accurately.

The Chairman of the board is its senior member. His responsibility is to look after the interests of the company's shareholders who in turn, as owners of the company, are the final source of authority. The Managing Director is the chief executive director and he has the responsibility for the day-to-day operation of the company. His is a position of great power, and often vulnerability. When the Chairman reports to the shareholders it is usually the Managing Director who must carry the can for lack of profitability.

There is no Wages Council for directors; they tend to be among the best paid people in Britain since many people are directors of a large number of different company's. (Hugh Nicholson has the record for the most directorships. In 1961 he held 458.) The following survey sets out median earnings for directors by industrial group, for a respresentative sample of British industries. 90 per cent of the companies surveyed would be considered small (turnover less than £50 million per year). Earnings in larger companies are considerably more.

| | Annual Average Earnings | | |
Type of Industry	Chairman £ per year	Managing Director £ per year	Other Directors £ per year
Chemicals	27,300	20,020	22,500
Food, drink and tobacco	23,000	22,800	21,300
Metal manufacture	26,387	19,800	17,146
Professional services	20,500	20,500	19,500
Construction	21,600	20,000	17,500

	Annual Average Earnings		
	Chairman	Managing Director	Other Directors
	£ per year	£ per year	£ per year
Textiles	20,000	20,000	19,000
Insurance, banking, finance and business services	19,750	20,200	18,800
Paper, printing & publishing	21,000	20,000	16,000
Electrical engineering	20,000	20,000	15,600
Computer services	-	17,485	23,375
Timber, furniture	20,000	18,000	17,150
Other manufacturing industries	18,000	18,720	16,800
Distribution trades	16,398	19,300	16,500
Clothing and footwear	-	20,300	18,165
Mechanical engineering	18,200	19,350	14,150
Miscellaneous services	17,900	17,500	16,000
Instrument engineering	-	21,000	14,000
Transport and communications	15,250	15,250	15,850
Bricks, pottery, clay and cement	-	18,000	14,750

Perhaps more fascinating, though less representative, are some of the salaries drawn by company
chairmen in the appropriate year given below.

		£	
British Petroleum	Sir David Steel	120,385	1979
Shell	P. Baxendell	110,915	1979
Ford	Sir Francis Beckett	76,431	1978
ICI	Sir Maurice Hodgson	124,380	1980
Trafalgar House	N. Broackes	58,000	1980
Associated Newspapers	Lord Rothermere	66,443	1980
Allied Breweries	K.S. Showering	69,474	1980
Guinness	The Earl of Iveagh	13,300	1980
Whitbread	C.H. Tidbury	41,961	1980
Grand Metropolitan	Maxwell Joseph	17,262	1980
Imperial Group	Sir John Pile	68,000	1980
Anglia Television	Marquess of Townshend and Raynham	17,693	1979
Harlech Television	Lord Harlech	14,242	1980
Pearson Longman	M.J. Hare*	1,649	1979
Collins	W.J. Collins	35,000	1979
EMI	Sir John Read	50,803	1979

*(In the same year S. Pearson and Son paid
£62,805 to its highest paid director. M.J. Hare
was then managing director of this parent
company.)

		£	
GEC	Lord Nelson of Stafford	45,000	1979
Lonhro	Lord Duncan-Sandys	38,000	1978
Marks and Spencer	Sir Marcus Sieff	64,077	1980

Managing directors do not always publish their salary in the company's accounts, although the remuneration for the highest paid director is stated.

MANAGERS

Managers direct and control the business of a company. But there are hundreds of thousands of managers in Britain; they can't all be doing the same things. Perhaps the best way to categorise them is by department within a company. These departments are associated with different functions and tasks that are quite recognisable. Each of these functions is examined separately in another section. For now, however, the different departments are set out below along with a brief description, within each department. Three positions are listed: the first, Department Head, is the person who is responsible for the entire department. They are often directors of the company. The second, Assistant Manager, is usually in charge of one or more divisions within the department (such as market research under Advertising). They would take over in the absence of the Department Head. The Third, Supervisor, is responsible for a particular work group of which he may be part - such as head draughtsman in a design department.

These positions exist in almost every company, although the job titles may vary. The figures quoted below represent average annual salaries for these position, by department. The value of perks and fringe benefits is not included. From these, one can get some idea of the importance of the various functions within a company as well as the market for different skills.

Investment/Capital Projects
Administers the company's funds, estimates the costs and returns on various undertakings and advices the directors on them.

	£ per year
Department Head	22,500
Assistant Manager	13,500
Supervisor	11,700

Corporate Planning
Makes recommendations on the company's long-term policies and offers advice on how to achieve them. The planning and investment departments work closely together.

	£ per year
Department Head	22,500
Assistant Manager	11,100
Supervisor	10,100

Advertising
Forms and directs the company's marketing policy.They often work closely with outside advertising agencies.

	£ per year
Department Head	21,600
Assistant Manager	10,800
Supervisor	9,400

Accounting
Manages the company's accounts. These top positions are filled by Chartered Accountants.

	£ per year
Department Head	18,000
Assistant Manager	14,000
Supervisor	11,500

Sales

Directs the company's sales force. The general approach may be set by advertising, but the response is generated by the sales department. Bonuses may be more important in this department than in others.

	£ per year
Department Head	18,000
Assistant Manager	11,500
Supervisor	10,200

Research and Development

Plans and directs the work of engineers and scientists. Their work is directed toward finding more efficient techniques and better products. These positions are often filled by engineers.

	£ per year
Department Head	17,100
Assistant Manager	11,000
Supervisor	9,900

Purchasing

Directs the work of wholesale and material buyers in an effort to manage stocks and minimise costs.

	£ per year
Department Head	16,750
Assistant Manager	11,500
Supervisor	10,375

Production

Responsible for setting and meeting production targets, along with the policies of the Board of Directors.

	£ per year
Department Heads	16,500
Assistant Managers	11,500
Supervisor	10,000

Company Secretary

Makes certain that the company abides by the relevant statues in its operation. The top position is often filled by a solicitor.

	£ per year
Department Head	16,000
Assistant Manager	10,500
Supervisor	8,000

Personnel

Plans and administers policies regarding pay, conditions and staffing. Industrial relations duties are sometimes included.

	£ per year
Department Head	15,500
Assistant Manager	11,200
Supervisor	9,500
Recruitment Officer	7,500
Training Officer	8,100

Public Relations

Sometimes combined with advertising, this department is responsible for enhancing the company's public image.

	£ per year
Department Head	15,000
Assistant Manager	9,000
Supervisor	8,200

Quality Control
Conducts tests and devises ways of maintaining quality standards in production. The top position is sometimes filled by an engineer.

	£ per year
Department Head	12,500
Assistant Manager	10,000

Research
In some companies, this is just the Library staff. It is responsible for maintaining resources used by other departments – particularly planning – in their decision making.

	£ per year
Department Head	10,000
Assistant	7,000

PERSONNEL MANAGERS
These managers develop and administer the policies that bear on recruiting and retaining an adequate labour force; wage and salary structure, benefits, working coditions, and work rules. The magnitude of these duties depends on the size of the company and its labour force. Personnel managers in small companies would earn just under £10,000 per year, while those in the largest companies would earn about £28,000 per year. In banking, for example, the average salary is £16,500 per year.

SALES REPRESENTATIVES/EXECUTIVES
Sales is perhaps the most difficult occupation about which to generalise. What one does and earns depends entirely on what one sells, where it is sold, and the individual relationship with the employer. The earnings of the door to door salesman can hardly be compared to those of the

international arms dealer, however, all salesmen have some essential things in common whether they are self employed or part of a company's force. They seek out customers, solicit orders, and provided explanations and advice about their products. The distinction between sales representatives and shop assistants is that the former find customers with whom they then maintain a close relationship, while the latter wait for the customers to come to them.

Sales representatives employed as part of a marketing team are usually paid a base salary that is a relatively small percentage of their expected earnings – around 70 per cent. Supervisors establish the volume of sales that constitute the representative's 'target' or quota – that which the employer is planning to sell. The representative will earn a commission on the volume of sales up to and including that target. If the target should be exceeded, the represent-ative will usually be paid a higher rate of commission or will receive a bonus. It is quite common for these bonuses to be in kind rather than in cash. Bonuses in the form of travel or holidays are the most common. Representatives' earnings, therefore, can vary a great deal and may not depend entirely on their own efforts. Those stuck with selling bad products or with impoverished clients will find it more difficult to earn their commissions. Supervisors usually make allowances for these problems, though, and a representative assigned to a particularly difficult customer route is likely to be given a higher base rate of pay.

Sales executives are essentially the managers who supervise and direct teams of representatives. They may also be involved in planning marketing strategies.

According to the Institute of Sales Management, the best-paid sales executives (representatives, supervisors, and managers) in Britain last year were those selling computer hardware. Median earnings were £15,000 per year, but the best of those were earning upwards of £57,500 per year. Those in computer software (programmes, etc.) were next with median earnings of £13,550. Office equipment came third at £12,250 and insurance fourth at £12,200. The worst-paid executives were those who sold domestic appliances. Their median earnings were £7,075 per year. The following figures are median earnings - including commissions and cash bonuses - for sales positions by their rank within a company's marketing operation.

	Median Earnings
Managing Director	15,000
Director	12,000
Sales Manager	10,192
Marketing Manager	9,650
UK Sales Manager	10,000
Export Sales Manager	10,000
Special Accounts Manager	8,950
Regional Sales Manager	10,650
Area Sales Manager	8,500
Branch Manager	8,020
Office Manager	8,175
Sales Representative	7,250
Sales Engineer	7,380
(technical sales)	

The figure for Sales Representative, numerically the most important position, is remarkably close to the estimate in the New Earnings Survey of £7,150 per year.

Perks and fringe benefits are very good for sales executives as a group – perhaps better than for any other department in a company. Sales representatives almost always get a company car, and sales executives are more likely to get one than are any other group. Other perks are at the same level or are slightly better than for other executives. The Institute reports that overnight allowances averaged about £25 and dinner allowances between £6 and £7.

The following figures are average earnings for positions in retail sales – selling directly to the customer.

Salesmen/Shop Assistants

Work in shops and serve customers as they come in. Commissions as a percentage of income will vary depending on what they sell; expensive items (furniture, appliances) generally come with higher commissions. The New Earnings Survey estimates weekly earnings of about £90 for all these positions. Those in retail food or stationery departments, for example, would earn about £70 per week while furniture salesmen might earn £110.

Roundsmen

Deliver and sell goods at households and small shops. This job is usually associated with food – the milkman or the baker's van driver. These positions are much like shop assistants in that the roundsmen usually just take orders and keep track of inventory: they rarely seek out new business themselves. Average earnings here about about £105 per week for roundsmen dealing in food.

Driver-salesmen/Van salesmen

Sells goods (usually food) to consumers from a van parked on the street. Earnings vary with the seasons and with the weather. Some van salesmen switch products during the year or take up different employment. Unsocial hours (weekends and nights) are the peak hours for van salesmen who can earn £130 per week in London when they work a full week – about 40 hours spread over six days.

DISTRIBUTION SPECIALISTS

Distribution managers are experts in coordinating and transporting goods between markets. Employers are specialised shipping and haulage firms or the distribution departments of manufacturing concerns. Job titles vary, but the most common ones are Depot or Warehouse Manager, Transport Engineer, or Import/Export Manager. Suprisingly, very few of these jobs are in the London area; most are in the North West.

	£ per year
Distribution Directors (Set policy)	16,000
Senior Managers (Implement policy)	9,900
Technical Experts (Schedule & Route Planners)	8,300
Depot Managers (Supervise drivers, etc.)	6,500

CLERICAL WORK

London is by far the most important market for secretarial and clerical workers, and the salaries below represent an average for jobs in the London area. These figures are therefore inclusive of London weighting which averages about £650 per annum for inner areas and £325 per annum for jobs in outer London. The term clerical work covers jobs with a range of skills and responsibilities. At higher levels, these jobs require supervisory and decision—making ability. The salary range below reflects in part this difference within jobs with the same titles and in part pay increases that come with seniority.

	£ per week
Clerical Assistant	54.00 − 89.00
Typists	52.00 − 95.00
Shorthand/Audio Typist	54.00 − 102.00
Word Processors	80.00 − 90.00

	£ per year
Personal Secretaries	5,000 − 7,000
Typing Superintendents	7,100 − 8,400
PAYE Clerk	3,800 − 5,500
Payroll Clerks	4,400
Senior Payroll Clerks	4,800
Microfilm Operator	4,000
Senior Microfilm Operator	4,175
Duplicating Manager	4,300
Key Punch Supervisor	5,150

Perks: In the London area, free transport (travel tickets) and subsidised meals (luncheon vouchers) are common benefits.
The following are basic rates for experienced secretaries by region.*

	£ per week
London	86.50
Reading	67.75
Basingstoke	67.50
Birmingham	67.25
Crawley	67.25
Edinburgh	67.25
Leicester	67.25
Manchester	67.25
Oxford	67.00

	£ per week
Brighton	66.75
Coventry	66.75
Bristol	66.50
Glasgow	66.50
Wolverhampton	66.50
Leeds	66.25
Newcastle	65.75
Northampton	65.75
Cardiff	65.50
Nottingham	65.50
Portsmouth	65.25
Sheffield	65.25
Southend	65.25
Liverpool	65.00
Middlesborough	65.00
Southampton	65.00
Stoke-on-Trent	64.00

TEMPORARY CLERICAL WORKERS

These workers are employed by agencies who then match their skills with part-time work in nearby offices. The agency charges these offices a fee which exceeds the wage paid to the temporary employees; the difference is the agency's income, from 15 to 30 per cent of their charges. The following hourly rates of pay are for experienced temporaries. Actual hours of work, though, are likely to be very irregular.

	Central London £ per hour	Oxford £ per hour
Senior Secretary	3.25 – 3.58	2.08 – 2.29
Secretary	2.87 – 3.18	1.96 – 2.17
Audio Typist	2.69 – 2.97	1.97 – 2.06
Copy Typist	2.25 – 2.47	1.72 – 1.86
Clerk	1.67 – 2.25	1.41 – 1.86

GIRL/GUY FRIDAY

The main characteristic of this job is the range of duties that it might include. Employees are usually thought of as wide-ranging personal assistants able to do secretarial work as well as arrange a reception. Annual salaries in central London are around £5,000 per year but can go higher depending on the responsibilities involved.

EMPLOYMENT AGENTS

Employment agents match applicants to jobs. They receive a percentage of the applicant's annual salary when a client is successfully placed.This varies from 5 to 15 per cent. The difficulty of their task depends on the state of the job market; it becomes increasingly difficult when jobs are scarce and fewer vacancy notices are sent to them. Most employment agents are large firms rather than individuals. The firm's income depends on how many applicants it can place. Its employees are essentially clerical workers paid an annual salary.

TRANSLATOR/INTERPRETER

A translator converts printed matter from one language to another; an interpreter does the same for the spoken word. Translators working in the private sector earn between £18 and £25 per 1000 words, depending on the languages. French translated to English, for example, pays only £18; Russian to English would pay £25 because there are fewer people who can do it, and they are often in great demand. In the Civil Service, the Linguist Specialist Class does much of the translation work for government departments.
The salary at the entry level of this grade is £4,900 per year rising through promotion to £8,900 per year. Translators are often called

upon to convert the spoken word into print of another language – at conferences, for example. Simultaneous interpreters convert the spoken word of one language into the spoken word of another and have this field entirely to themselves. Simultaneous interpreters employed by large, mutli-national companies would earn average salaries between £9 and 11,000 per year. Some business services such as management consultants, will provide these interpretors, charging a daily fee of around £50.

BANKING

Finance has always been an important industry in Britain, and the banking business has been especially influential, particularly in foreign trade and development. There are, essentially, three types of banks. Clearing banks or retail banks service individual customers and are the type that most poeple would recognise through their local branch offices. Merchant banks serve business and corporate clients and offer advice on investments and financial policy. Foreign banks and consortium banks have branches in the U.K. to conduct international business. As manufacturing declines, many are looking to banking for the creation of new jobs. It has been a successful industry, even during the current recession, as evidenced by the average salary increase of about 17 per cent since last year. Jobs differ across these groups, but they are similar enough to permit generalisations about salaries in the industry. The following jobs are common to the big banks which operate in the financial district – the City of London.

General Manager

This is the top position in a bank – often called Managing Director in smaller banks or Senior Vice-President in an international branch office. The median salary for this job is around £35,000 per year, but the pay varies greatly according to the size of the bank. The General Manager of a large operation could easily earn £60 - 80,000 per year.

Foreign Exchange/Money Managers
This is the cornerstone of any banking operation, and it must be filled by a qualified manager in order for the bank to receive permission to open its doors. The person in this jobs oversees financial relations with other banks. Only top people in the banking business get into these positions, and the pay averages between £28 - 36,000 per year. It can go much higher for someone with the right mix of experience and connections.

Assistant Managers
Usually run a department, such as Corporate Relations. Also known as Assistant Directors or Senior Managers, these jobs come with an average salary of about £24,000 per year which will vary depending on the nature of the department.

Loan Managers
Are really the Assistant Managers in charge of loans. Specifically, they would oversee normal lending operations with corporate customers, leaving specialised areas like ship finance to others. The average salary here is also around £24,000 per year and is less likely to vary than in other jobs.

Bond Issue Managers
Also known as Investment Managers, these experts organise efforts to raise capital for clients through issue of bonds. Bond Issue Manager must be well versed in and well connected with the

financial markets. The demand for these jobs is currently very high, as are salaries — averaging around £28,000 per year. The best of these managers will earn £38 - £40,000.

Corporate Finance Executives
These positions are usually associated with Merchants Banks. They provide clients with advice on mergers, acquisitions and corporate financial policy. Salaries average around £23,000 per year.

Foreign Exchange Dealers
One step below Foreign Exchange manager. The average salary is around £21,000 per year.

Financial Controllers
This position is usually filled by a Chartered Accountant who manages the bank's books, much like in any other business. The average salary across all banks is around £20,000 per year, but Financial Controllers in larger banks can earn close to £30,000.

Project Finance Directors
These experts are brought in at the beginning of a large project, such as the construction of a new plant — to organise and provide advice on finance. The nature of this work is similar to management consulting, and the Project Finance Directors are, like consultants, paid set fees. Obviously, earnings will vary according to the number and size of projects one takes on, but the average is around £17,000 per year.

Senior Lending Officers
Are the ones who go around and find loans for the bank to make. They report directly to the Loan Manager and earn around £15,000 per year.

Branch Managers

This rather confusing title means different things in different types of banks. In foreign banks, it means the U.K. Director of Operations who would earn close to £24,000 per year. A branch manager in a clearing bank, however, is responsible for one of the thousands of branches scattered throughout Britain. His pay would vary with the size of his operation. A branch manager with 50 or 60 employees (in the West End of London, for example), would earn over £20,000 per year. Managers of the smallest operations earn at least £10,000 per year.

Bond Dealers

Work directly for Bond Issue Managers and earn from £14 to £20,000 per year.

Syndication Managers

When a bank takes on a very big loan, the Syndication Manager attempts, in a sense, to subcontract at least part of the loan to other banks so reduce the risk of default on the first bank. These managers average about £14,000 per year, but banks spreading out big loans will pay them more - closer to £20,000 per year.

Documentary Credits Managers

Establish the authenticity of trading documents - certificates of origin, bills of lading, etc., - for goods involved in loans. Sometimes, a Loans Documentation Officer will take on this task in addition to his usual responsibility of over-seeing the legality of loan documents. Pay will average about £12,500 per year.

Investments Fund/Portfolio Managers
This job is associated with Merchant Banks who will manage and advise their clients' investments. It pays about £13,000 per year.

Banking Advisors
Provide advice on the banking scene in the City, usually to foreign banks trying to open branches there. The pay varies considerably, according to the advisor's connections, but averages around £12,500 per year. It is, however, only a temporary job.

Top-Level Clerical Staff
Those who have been in the banking business for several years perform functions usually associated with junior executives and are paid £8 – 10,000 per year.

It is difficult to assess what the most senior bankers earn but in 1979 Lord Armstrong, chairman of the Midland Bank, was paid £59,606 while in the same year the highest paid director of Barclays received £60,000. The merchant bank Hill Samuel paid their most valuable director £64,000 in 1978.

Perks: It is widely held that banking industry offers its employees the best benefits in Britain. Informed sources value the total benefit package at 40 – 50 per cent of the employee's salary. The most important perk and the one peculiar to banking is cheap loans. People who work in coal mines get cheap coal: people who work in banks get cheap money. Banks will lend employees an amount about four times their annual salary at interest rates around 5 per cent. The rate on older loans is about three per cent. These loans are supposed to be used for housing.

Alternatively, banks will subsidise outside
mortgages. Interest-free loans for public
transport tickets are also provided. Of course,
the value of this cheap money depends on the
normal interest rate as well as how big a loan
one takes. Most banks also provide health care
benefits for employees and their families, as
well as a generous pension plan. There are also
bonus plans, and, for senior management,
arrangements for company cars.

Senior Bank employees, particularly of merchant
banks, are often directors of the businesses
which they finance. Although salaries rarely come
with these duties the supply of additional perks
is not unusual.

BUREAU DE CHANGE
Rates of pay are set by a central office
according to the size of each operation which, in
turn, determines the manager's responsibilities
and workload.

	£ per year
Managers (smallest shops)	5 - 6,000
(largest shops)	8 -11,000
Cashiers	4 - 5,000

Not surprisingly, the work and conditions are
much like those in a bank, although the perks for
management are about average - below those of
banks.

STATISTICIANS
Most of the jobs cited as 'statistician' are
filled by people who have combined their
knowledge of statistics with other skills. By far
the best explanation of their salaries is that
other skill. In the few cases where they are

hired strictly for their statistical skills – such as when they leave university – they are paid about the same salary as economists. Head of a statistics department in a large corporation earns about £17,000 per year.

RESEARCHERS

What a researcher is paid depends a great deal on what is being researched and especially on the skills that are necessary for the work. University researchers are sometimes paid on lecturer scales, sometimes on clerical scales depending on their qualifications. The going rate for full-time researchers without graduate training is around £4,500 per year. Casual work is paid about £2 per hour. The following scales are for research workers in the Civil Service (outside the sciences). These employees are usually already trained in their fields.

	£ per year
Research Officers	4,900 – 6,950
Senior Research Officers	7,787 – 9,517
Economic Assistants, Assistant Statisticians	4,900 – 6,745
Senior Economic Assistants, Statisticians	6,950 – 8,555

The hours of work are 36 per week in London, 37 elsewhere. The allowance is £780 per year for inner London and £325 for outer London.

HEAD-HUNTERS/PERSONNEL CONSULTANTS

These experts are essentially employment agents for executives. The main difference between head-hunters and employment agents is that the former actually search to find executives for firms or positions for clients. The search for executives probably means recruiting someone who leaves his position in one firm for a similar position in another - usually at higher pay. The consultants who do this work are paid for their information - particularly their contacts within a given occupation. These consultants usually specialise in one occupation, often one in which they themselves worked. Earnings come from fees paid by companies when the consultant fills a vacancy or as a percentage of annual salary when they find a position for applicants. Directors or partners in personnel consulting agencies earn about £25 - 30,000 per year. Agencies expect them to have a wealth of personal contacts from which to work and employees are often therefore recruited from the ranks of executives who have retired from some other profession. Managing associates supervise searches through trade journals, etc., but are less likely to have as thorough a network of contacts. They earn between £10 and £20,000 per years some of that through commissions and bonuses. This career is one that can be entered only after a certain amount of experience in the business world.

OPERATIONS RESEARCH

Employees in this field study problems of allocation and use of resources - personnel as well as materials. They devise ways of getting around these problems and making operations more efficient.

Operations Research Manager

These employees use mathematical techniques and models to simulate management problems (such as the maintenance of adequate stocks) and to discover their solutions. A great deal of this work is now done on computers. Operations research personnel are often located in planning or production departments. The head of an

operations research section will average about
£13,000 per year across all companies.

Work Study Managers

These managers analyse the way in which jobs are
performed to determine which methods are the most
efficient. They are sometimes known as time and
motion officers because of their interest in the
movements used and the speed at which jobs are
performed, as well as for their ubiquitious
stopwatch. This position would be within an
operations research section. Work study managers
assist those in the production department to set
output quotas. Annual salaries would average just
under £9,000 per year.

ADVERTISING

Employees in advertising develop marketing
strategies and direct sales activities for a
company. While many companies have their own
advertising departments, most make use of outside
advertising agencies. The following figures are
representative of salaries in the larger agencies.
Bonuses seem to be particularly important here.

Marketing Manager
Brand/Product Manager

These managers are part of a company's staff. They
formulate general marketing policies for a range
of products and adjudicate between the ideas of
their minions. Salaries average about £10,000 per
year.

Account Executive

This is the 'bright idea' person in an advertising
agency who develops campaigns for clients and
directs their development. Salaries for those with
about 5 years experience would be £12 - 13,000 per
year. Those at board level earn about £17,000.

Traffic/Production Executive

Co-ordinates the artwork and copy writing for advertisements. Salaries are between £7 - 8,000 per year.

Art Directors

In charge of the agency's artists and the work they produce on a range of campaigns. Art directors are also involved in tranlsating concepts into designs. Salaries betwen £20 - 25,000 are common.

Copywriters

Write advertising copy, sometimes developing basic ideas, sometimes taking them from the account executives. Copywriters often do freelance work and are kept on retainers by a number of agencies. Those who run their own agencies can earn up to £50,000 per year.

MARKETING ANALYSTS

Are researchers, often with knowledge of demographics and statistics, who estimate the demand for new products and the reception for different advertising approaches. Those working for companies average about £9,000 per year; those working for specialist agencies can earn twice that.

BUYERS
(Wholesale/Retail)

Buyers purchase goods and materials from other producers for immediate resale or processing before resale. Their compensation depends entirely on what they are buying - particularly the quantity involved. In a general department store, for example, there would be one buyer for each department; in chain stores, a Central Buyer would purchase hardware, for every store in the chain.

Retail Buyers earn about £9,000 per year; Central Buyers about £13,000. Both travel a great deal in order to make purchases.

PUBLICITY OFFICER/PRESS OFFICER
Part of a public relations staff, these members deal specifically with the media in an attempt to secure promotion and publicity for a particular enterprise or operation. Pay varies with the nature of the employer; those in the theatre, where pay is generally low, average around £6,500 per year; those in business closer to £9,000.

CHAPTER SEVEN

Tradesmen and Manual Workers

MANUAL WORKERS

When considering the pay of manual workers it is as well to bear in mind that this group often receive substantially more than the basic rate for their work. As well as overtime, systems of bonuses, shift payments and payments by result operate, in all combinations. When all these factors are taken into account, it is interesting to note that they account for over a quarter of total earnings.

Many argue that the workers' interest in output-related pay really developed while government incomes policies were in force and these extra payments became a way of increasing earnings without violating the restraints. Management's interest is obvious. Such payments create incentives to increase output.

Besides overtime, there are two important sources of output-related earnings. The first is payment-by-results. This system establishes a relationship between workers' (or work group's) output and their pay, in the form of an addition to basic rates. Sometimes they operate only after output has exceeded some basic target rate. In this sense, it is much like a bonus which is paid for exceptional performance. Piece rates are an extreme form of payment-by-results, the essential difference being one of degree; piece rate payments contribute the majority of worker's earnings. Their use has declined in Britain. Altogether payments-by-results systems apply to about 40 per cent of British manual workers and workers and contribute close to 8 per cent of their total earnings.

The other major source of output-related earnings is shift pay. These are premium rates or bonuses paid for undertaking work that is less pleasant than usual: dangerous work, work at a faster pace, work during unsocial hours, and so on. Shift premiums are paid to about 23 per cent of manual workers and account for over 3 per cent of average earnings.

The following chart sets out the influence of payment-by-results and shift premium pay on total earnings for various occupations. For most non-manuals, the influence is insignificant.

	% Of Earnings From Payments-By-Results	% Of Earnings From Shift Payments
Managers (other than general management)	2.4	0.5
Clerical Work	1.3	2.2
Sales	16.8	0.7
Personal Services (catering, cleaning, etc.)	4.5	4.0
Farming and Fishing	7.5	0.3
Materials Processing	7.9	6.3

	% Of Earnings From Payments-By-Results	% Of Earnings From Shift Payments
Making and Repairing (printing, woodwork)	12.5	2.6
Processing and making (metals and electricals)	8.4	3.1
Painting, packaging	9.2	3.3
Construction and making	16.3	1.1
Transport	7.7	3.4

PERKS FOR MANUAL WORKERS

These benefits are sometimes known as allowances. They are a valuable form of compensation which serve as aids in recruitment. Like management's perks, allowances are often in-kind payments which are not taxed. Many of these benefits also arose during incomes policy periods as means of increasing compensation without violating restrictions on pay increases. Some benefits, though, may actually be cheaper for the company to provide than for workers to purchase individually - such as transport by company commuting buses. Allowances vary between industries, jobs and firms, but the following list sets out some of the more common ones and their approximate values.

Meal and Food Allowances

Many companies provide luncheon vouchers or subsidised canteens for their employees. The latter has an advantage to management in that it cuts down on the amount of time workers need to get to and from lunch. Subsidies vary but usually equal about 25 - 50 per cent of costs (including service).Employees who are away from work on company business often have their lunch expenses met by the employer; those who are usually away – like drivers – receive a fixed lunch allowance, usually around £1.25. Allowances for evening meals are often combined with overnight allowances of around £7 – £10.

Breaks for Meals and Tea

Firms provide breaks for meals and for tea, and while most pay for the time spent on tea breaks, very few pay for meal time (usually lunch hour). Two tea breaks of 10 minutes each is about the norm, while the lunch break varies from 30 to 60 minutes.

Travel Allowances

These allowances are less common and apply only when workers are travelling on company business. When they are, the company usually reimburses the cost of rail fares or provides a mileage rate of 12 to 25 pence per mile when the worker uses his own car. Employers also provide assistance in getting to work when they face difficulties attracting enough workers. It is common in these cases to provide company buses which run to outlying areas and charge one half or a quarter of operating costs.

Allowances for Safety Clothing

Where work is dangerous and requires protective clothing, the employer usually provides the footwear, clothing or safety glasses. Most companies also provide or pay for cleaning of protective clothing. These arrangements are not the same as those where the employer requires workers to wear uniforms merely for the sake of appearance. In the latter case, the employer is much less likely to provide an allowance.

Tool Allowances

These are paid only when the employee provides

his own tools — usually simple ones. Where this is the case, the employer is likely to reimburse the worker's purchase cost.

Allowances for Training

Where workers undertake training that the employer sees as beneficial to the company's interest, time off from work may be permitted (usually with pay) to attend the course. Some assistance with travel costs may also be provided. In a few cases, workers may receive a supplement or bonus when they complete the training. These arrangements are far more common for clerical workers than for manuals.

COAL MINERS

Miners have traditionally been among the highest paid manual workers in industry — the highest by industry group. This year, earnings for underground miners are second only to newspaper printers. The recent increases in the price of oil — and with it the price of coal — have improved the economic situation of the industry and with it the earnings of miners.

	Total	£ per week Before Overtime, Shift & Payments By Results
Underground Workers	154.80	103.30
Surface Workers	126.70	85.20

Perks: Some mines provide free or reduced price coal.

ENGINEERING

Engineering is quite rightly thought of as the most important industry in Britain — no doubt because it groups together a great number of different products in its description. Traditionally, engineering works have provided the bulk of Britain's manufactured exports. There are a great number of jobs within the industry that are also found elsewhere – particularly in related fields such as shipbuilding. The highest paid workers, in maintenance, also work the most overtime (about 6 hours per week).Within engineering there are of course many craft and trade workers. For them pay varies by the type of engineering – partly because of the nature of the work and partly because some engineering groups are most profitable than others.

| | £ Per Week | | |
	Skilled	Semi-Skilled	Labourers
Mechanical	108.40	94.50	81.50
Electrical	113.50	91.80	85.80
Motor Vehicle	117.60	102.10	92.80
Aerospace	126.85	107.50	95.10

Pay also varies by region:

	Skilled	Semi-Skilled	Labourers
South East	113.00	102.80	87.00
East Anglia	106.70	90.00	77.40
South West	113.30	95.00	82.20
West Midlands	111.70	90.60	80.70
East Midlands	117.90	100.00	82.60

| | £ Per Week | | |
	Skilled	Semi-Skilled	Labourers
Yorkshire and Humberside	107.50	91.80	81.40
North West	115.90	103.00	88.00
North	112.20	95.00	96.60
Wales	111.00	96.70	89.30
Scotland	121.85	97.70	91.30

These jobs are common in engineering, but it should also be borne in mind that actual earnings in engineering are about 25 per cent above basic rates. Chances for overtime and piecework are not, however, the same in all these jobs.

	£ per week Basic Rates
Assemblers	85.00
Boilermen	82.20
Cleaners	73.50
Coppersmiths	98.70
Crane Drivers	86.50
Diecasters	68.00
Engine Tenders	65.00
Extruder Operators	67.00
Finishers (Painted Metal)	94.00
Floorsweepers	80.40
Fitters	80.00
Grinders	67.40
Line Stock Feeders	95.20
Loose Pattern Moulders	78.70
Material Handlers	77.90
Millwrights	100.00
Moulding Machine Operators	67.00
Patternmakers	82.00
Polishers	65.00
Press Operators	67.00
Quality Control Inspectors	101.00
Scrapcutters	70.00
Shotblasters	85.00
Solderers	93.00
Spray Operators	95.00
Toolmakers	98.00
Platers	114.00
Welders	115.00
Other Boilermakers (riveters and caulkers)	114.50
Shipwrights	112.00
Joiners	114.00

Perks: There is an allowance of one third basic rates for hours worked on a night shift.

BUILDING

A great number of different crafts appear under the general heading of building trades, represented by an equal variety of unions. The pay of carpenters, say, might be more closely related to a cabinet maker elsewhere than to the plumber working next to him on a site. Some of the more commmon construction and building jobs are listed below. It is important to bear in mind that work is unlikely to be available all year round.

	£ Per Week	
	Total Earnings	Basic Rates
Bricklayers	109.00	76.80
Carpenters and Joiners	105.90	77.70
Craftsmens' Mates	93.60	67.10
Foremen	125.00	97.00
Gas Fitters	131.60	89.50
Labourers in Civil Engineering	100.50	72.30
Painters and Decorators	98.90	75.60
Plasterers	98.10	76.60
Plumbers and Pipefitters	118.60	88.80
Sewermen and Pipe Joiners	111.80	77.50
Sheet Metal Workers	115.20	89.50
Steel Erectors, Scaffolders	141.80	85.80
Welders (skilled)	121.80	88.00

Perks: Under certain conditions, workers are guaranteed a week's wages if work is halted for reasons beyond the control of the parties.

Other positions in the building industry:

	£ per year
Purchasing Managers	6,400 – 8,000
Estimate Assessors	7,500 – 10,000
Contract/Subcontract Managers	9,400 – 12,800

HEATING AND VENTILATION WORKERS

These jobs involve the construction and installation of ventilation, heating, and air conditioning equipment.

	£ per week
Craft apprentices	34.50
(at age 20)	79.00
Mates over age 18	79.00
Assistants	88.60
Improvers	93.50
Fitters	98.60
Advanced Fitters	119.00
Chargehands	123.00
Foremen	128.00

These are special allowances of 12 – 24p per hour for welding, 47p per hour for exposed work at heights over 125 feet, and 12p per hour for work on ladders. In addition, there is an allowance of £1.18 per day for work under abnormal conditions.

LIFT AND ESCALATOR ERECTORS

These workers install and renovate escalators and lifts. The skills involved are essentially those of engineering, with the emphasis on electrical work. The following are basic rates for these jobs. Overtime, bonuses, and shift payments, will raise earnings about 12 per cent above these rates.

	£ per week
Mates	79.40
Improvers	93.80

	£ per week
After 1 year	94.60
Trained Fitters	95.40
Advanced Fitters	100.30
Senior Fitters	110.20

The London allowance is £5.40 per week.

STEEPLEJACKS

In London:

	£ Per Week
Steeplejacks	107.52
Steeplejacks' Mates	93.90
Lightning Conductor Fitters	98.40
Lightning Conductor Fitters' Mates	88.70
Adult Learner (after 6 months)	80.60

FORESTRY WORKERS

The Forestry Commission manages Britain's forests and hires the relevant workers. Jobs are similar to those in construction work.

	£ Per Week
Workers (unskilled)	74.23
Gangers	86.40
Foremen	107.90
Camp Site Wardens	85.10
Rangers	89.00
Senior Rangers	107.90
Timber Forwarders	94.90

Perks: Under certain conditions, workers are paid for time lost because of bad weather. Exceptional work (e.g. very wet) is paid at premium rates.

BLACKSMITHS

Many blacksmiths are self-employed and travel around the farms and stables of their area, charging by the job or by the hour. Their earnings, therefore, vary according to the amount of work that they take on. The minimum hourly rate for blacksmiths is £1.65, but their charges will be considerably above that, reflecting the fact that much of their time is spent travelling. Average earnings will also vary by region because the type of work varies. Weekly earnings of about £90 are the norm.

LOCK, LATCH, AND KEY MAKERS

Workers in these jobs need metal working skills, particularly machine tool operators working within small tolerances. These skills are also in demand by other industries. Most lock and key manufacturers are based in the Midlands which is the centre for the engineering industry and the centre of demand for skilled tool workers. As a result, wages are quite high. Basic rates are listed below. Earnings can average 30-40 per cent above these rates

Machine Operators

	£ per week
Lowest grades (unskilled machine-tenders)	64.38
Highest grade (sample makers, etc.)	98.12

Payment-by-result systems are very important in this industry, frequently contributing as much as 25 per cent of total earnings.

LOCKSMITHS

The term locksmith encompasses a range of skills – from those who merely cut duplicate keys to

those who do security consulting for homes and
industries. Many locksmiths own their businesses
so that earnings come as net business receipts.
For normal jobs, they charge an hourly rate which
is about £15.

FARM LABOUR

Farming is often described as the oldest and most
vital of industries. There is no question that
it determines the lifestyle of its workers to a
greater extent than does any other industry, if
for no other reason than because farm workers
must live in rural areas - near the farm. Farm
labour tends to be extremely poorly paid. In part
this is because the work is unskilled and because
the profits to be divided between the farmer and
his labourers are low. It is also due to the
fact that employment relations are decentralised
and informal; half of all farms employ only one
worker, and many of these workers are part time.
For these reasons, the Agricultural Wages Board
was established to regulate pay. It sets out a
minimum rate of £78.30 per week for labourers
with some responsibility. Earnings do not
usually rise much above those minimums - perhaps
10 per cent - and most of that comes from
overtime hours rather than higher rates. The
following earnings are by work group.

	Wage Before Overtime Pay	Earnings
General Farm		
Workers	68.0	80.10
Machinery Drivers	69.80	90.50
Stockmen	76.40	91.50
Dairy Cowmen	88.00	108.00
Foremen	90.00	112.00

Earnings also vary by region - in part because of

different work associated with different crops raised in each area, also because labour market conditions vary.

	£ Per Week
North	82.20
Yorkshire and Humberside	80.20
East Midlands	84.80
East Anglia	84.40
South East	73.70
South West	87.00
West Midlands	80.00
North West	79.20
Wales	78.30

Perks: Farm labourers often receive free or reduced-price food, but the Agricultural Wages Board lets deductions be made for allowances in kind. Employers may deduct £3.62 from their worker's weekly wages when lodging is provided for the full week; £18.13 may be deducted for a full week's board.

GARDENERS/GROUNDSMEN
The distinction between groundsmen and gardeners varies between employers. One usually thinks of groundsmen as those who prepare and maintain playing fields while gardeners do the more ornamental work — particularly plant selection and landscaping. Where there are no playing fields, though, groundsmen are usually employed to do the heavier work (trimming and pruning, etc.) while the gardener might be responsible for raising plants in a greenhouse as well as supervising their arrangements. Groundsmen earn between £4,500 and £5,000 per year while gardeners average slightly more — around £5,100. Although some seasons are busier than others, both types of worker are employed all the year round.

TREE SURGEONS

Treat diseased trees and remove those that present some danger to property - dying trees that might fall on power lines, for example. The range of expertise within the field varies enormously, from those who simply prune and fell trees to experts on their diseases and their treatments. The work tends to be concentrated in urban areas. Local authorities are major employers. Average earnings here correspond to standard Local Authority pay scales, often with a premium for dangerous work (tree climbing), and average around £100 per week. Tree surgeons in the private sector operate as small businesses, taking their earnings in the form of business receipts. How much one earns, therefore, depends on the services one offers, as well as the quantity of work undertaken. Weekly earnings might average £110 - £130 per week, but the work is seasonal and the equipment expensive - at least, a lorry and plenty of ladders.

COOPERS

Coopers make and repair wooden tubs, vats and barrels. Journeymen coopers, who construct these vessels, earn a basic weekly rate of £77. Piecework and payments-by-results help to bring total earnings up to £100 per week. Daywork coopers do repair work. Their minimum weekly salary is £80 but the nature of their work raises earnings considerably. They receive an additional 33p per hour when called from the shop to conduct repairs as well as the chance for overtime earnings. Their total pay would be closer to £120 per week.

FURNITURE MAKERS

There is a great range of practice within furniture manufacture as to the way in which the pieces are constructed. Particularly in the construction of wooden furniture, the differences come down to the amount of handwork required. In large factories, much of the work is automated and the remainder is done with the use of machines. The following figures represent typical earnings for jobs in furniture manufacturing.

Veneer Makers:	£ per week
Operators	95.00
Woodworking machine operators	99.00

Construction	£ per week
Woodworking machinists (drill press operators, etc.)	99.00
Box makers	108.00
Joiners/carpenters	111.00
Painters/sprayers	99.00
Foremen	119.00

Skilled cabinet makers are often self-employed and charge by the piece for new or refinished work. In a factory, they might be employed to construct samples and design pieces. Their work is hand-work and their pay – about £120 per week.

PIANOFORTE MANUFACTURE/ORGAN BUILDING

	£ per hour
Pianoforte, skilled workers	1.92 (minimum)
Unskilled	1.63 (minimum)

	£ per week
Journeyman Organ Builders	70.20 (minimum)

Earnings are significantly above these rates, particularly for those who travel to make repairs. An independent piano tuner, for example,

will charge around £15 per hour for standard
work. Master organ builders are often self-
employed, constructing and renovating organs. They
would charge one fee for the whole operation.

TOY MAKERS

The Wages Council for Toy manufacturing has
established £49 per week as the minimum level of
pay for employees in its jurisdiction. Toy makers
are essentially wood and plastic workers. There
is a large proportion of part-time workers in the
labour force and a great deal of homework,
particularly in the simple, cheaper toys.

MATCH MAKERS

Those who make kitchen matches, not those who
arrange marriages. Basic pay begins at £66 per
week and rise to £84.25 for those in the highest
grades. Overtime will raise earnings about 30 per
cent above these rates.

AERATED WATER WORKERS

These workers make carbonated beverages and other
soft drinks under a Wages Council order which
sets the minimum weekly wage at £48. Some 25,000
workers are employed in this highly automated
industry, most of them as machine minders or
distributors. Union membership is quite low, but
earnings can be relatively high – especially in
the large organisations which dominate the
industry. Workers in the plant earn from £105 –
£110 per week; delivery drivers make about £95
per week while salesmen/distributors earn around
£115 (commissions can bring wages up to a much
higher level).

FLOUR MILLING

Milling has become a highly mechanised process
and job content tends to be similar to
manufacturing.

Day workers and   £73.45 per week
   statutory
   attendants

Perks: All workers have a guaranteed week including time lost from slack demand.

SUGAR CONFECTIONARY, COCOA, AND CHOCOLATE MAKERS

General Workers   £123.30 per week

Perks: Occasionally hot weather interferes with confectionary production, but at such times workers are protected against loss of earnings.

BUTCHERS/SLAUGHTERMEN

	£ per week
Butchers/meatcutters	82.00
Slaughtermen	80.00
Gutmen	78–80.00
Labourers	75–80.00

These earnings are for jobs in wholesale meat processing. Butchers in retail establishments can earn more – close to £90 per week.

BAKING

Over 100,000 people are employed in the baking industry, and, while the actual steps involved in bread and flour confectionary work are reasonably consistent, the character of the production process and the baking jobs varies with the size of the operation. Master bakers produce goods on a small scale, using traditional methods and selling them through their own outlets. Plant bakers mass produce goods using large-scale techniques and selling to retail distributors.

Basic rates of pay tend to be about the same in plant and master baker shops, although the variation in earnings (and in job content) is much greater in the latter.

The following jobs and weekly earnings are typical for workers in plant bakeries.

	£ per week
Pie Machine Operatives, Wrapping and Packing Operatives	74.00
Confectionary Finishers, Dough Makers and Recipe Weighers	99.00
Oven Controllers	105.00
Section Leader	112.00

The master baker is the person we usually think of as the baker. He is a self-employed business-man whose earnings are the profits of the business. Bakers are said to actually do rather well during recessions when people are more likely to treat themselves to a piece of confetionary. A small-town master baker with a single shop might earn between £7 - 10,000 from his business.

LEATHER/WOOL/ANIMAL SKINS
There are several different steps in the processing of pelts and skins, each of which is defined as a separate industry. Because each industry is small and the number of identifiable jobs is few, they are grouped together here in the order of the production process.

FELLMONGERING
Fellmongers remove the hair from animal skins, usually the wool from sheep skins. The wool is

then used to make rugs and the skins sent on for processing into garments.

	£ per week
Unskilled workers	75.00
Semi-skilled	77.50
Skilled workers	80–85.00

Piecework is very common in fellmongering.

HIDE AND SKIN TRADERS
The skill involved in these jobs is the ability to grade and judge animal hides and pelts on the basis of their potential use.

	£ per week
Labourers	80.00
	84.50
Classers (hides or skins)	88.00
Foremen/Head classers	91.50

The London allowance is 1p per hour.

TANNERS, CURRIERS AND DRESSERS
These workers take the hides and skins and turn them into leather. The initial cutting and shaping of the material takes place at this stage.

	£ per week
Unskilled workers (labourers)	78.00
Semi-skilled	83–87.00
Skilled workers	95–97.00

Piecework is also common here. In addition, shift work is often required, particularly in the more mechanised operations which often operate a continuous process.

INDUSTRIAL MANUFACTURE

This industry takes leather from the tanners and manufactures industrial goods — such as aprons and handles for equipment. The main difference between this work and similar work in textiles is that it is a bit more difficult to work with the material.

	£ per week
Unskilled workers	80.00
Semi-skilled	84.00
Skilled workers	95-100.00

LEATHER GOODS MANUFACTURE

These goods — such as purses and suitcases (but not clothing) — are produced in much the same way as are the industrial products above. The major difference is that the amount of fancy hand work tends to be greater. The earnings figures below do not apply to the specialist leather workers who produce custom goods sold through their own shops.

	£ per week
Basic rate workers (labourers, cutters)	87.00-90.00
Qualified workers (skilled)	93.00-101.00

WAREHOUSE WORKERS

Workers in these jobs, essentially, take goods and put them away. The skill comes in remembering where they were put. The difficulty of these jobs depends to a great extent on the type of stock one is handling. Explosives, for example, require more sensitive and skilled handling than bricks.

	£ per week
Packers	78.00
Loaders (heavy lifting)	82.00
Forklift drivers	105.00
Foreman/shipping clerks	120.00

SADDLERS
Saddlers, obviously, make saddles (sometimes other leather articles as well). Most of the firms in this industry are small, and there is a great deal of custom work which often sells at very high prices. The earnings below, however, are for saddlers engaged in standard production work.

£ Per Week

Semi-skilled workers (with four years experience)	90–95.00
Skilled workers	95–105.00

Real artisans, particularly those operating their own business, can earn £5–10.00 per hour. But the amount of work is unlikely to be constant.

MALT DISTILLING
Malting is the process of softening grain by steeping it in water to enhance fermentation and thus producing alcohol. The production process and character of the jobs comes close to that in the chemical industry. Virtually all of these jobs are in Scotland.

£ Per Week

General workers/floor maltsters	123.00
Boiler attendants and millers	125.00
Still operators and mash house attendants	128.00

Workers permanently on night shifts receive a 33 per cent premium on basic rates.

BESPOKE SHOEMAKERS/REPAIRERS

These jobs differ from those in footwear manufacturing in that they use traditional shoemaking skills; factory jobs in the bespoke shoemaking industry tend to be for machine operators and they are paid an average of £95 per week. Some jobs have higher rates of pay, which are set out below. Actual earnings can be as much as double these basic rates, largely because of payment-by-results schemes.

	£ per week
Foremen and managers	62.00
Sewing or stitching machine operators:	54.80 – 57.40
Press cutters responsible for cutting and costing	54.80 – 57.00
Makers of bespoke, including surgical, footwear	62.00
Clickers and Closers	55.60

	£ per week
Workers employed in altering footwear or on benching or finishing operations	54.50
Other workers	51.00

The familiar boot and shoe repairman on the corner is a self-employed businessman who charges by the job – not by the hour.

ARTIFICIAL LIMB MAKERS

These employees are highly skilled wood and metal workers. Their guaranteed hourly rate of pay rises from £2.06 to £2.33 for the highest skilled group. Most of the work is done by hand – especially the finishing. Earnings for these workers can be in excess of £130 per week

CLOTHING

Clothing has traditionally been one of Britain's most important industries, but in recent years much of the trade has been transferred to foreign manufacturers. Over 300,000 people still work in the garment industry. About 70 per cent of the total workforce are women. Wages tend to be low, and most of the industry is covered by Wages Councils. There has been a growth of small firms in recent years and a tendency to move away from the traditional textile centres — London and Leeds. The industry is usually subdivided according to the type of clothing being produced. These groups are reproduced below.

Ready-made and Wholesale Bespoke Tailoring

This industry is covered by a Wages Council order of the same name which sets out minimum weekly pay of £49.62. It is the largest single subsection of the clothing industry.

Dressmaking and Women's Light Clothing

Is covered by its own Wages Council order which sets out minimum weekly rates of £49.70. It is the second largest employer in the garment industry.

Shirt, Collar and Tie, Wholesale Mantle and Costume Corset Manufacturing

These industries each have their own Wages Councils which specify the same weekly rate — £49.62.

The jobs are approximately the same in these industries, as are their earnings. Most jobs involve some type of machine operation. Earnings for manual workers are about £85 per week.

Corset Makers

The Corset Manufacture Wages Council sets out minimum earnings of £49.62 per week for workers in this industry. The jobs tend to be the same as in other garment manufacturing, as are the earnings.

	£ per week
Packers	82.00
Machinists	90.00
Folders, press cutters	95.00
Markers and cutters	95.00

Glove Makers

About 4,500 employees work in the glove industry. While there is no Wages Council here, pay tends to be uniform across employers. The key division in this industry is between industrial and dress glove manufacture, the latter requiring more skill.

	£ per week
General workers (machine operators)	88.00
Glove webbers and block cutters	90–95.00
Leather dress glovemakers	95–103.00

Piecework is common in glovemaking as is custom work – especially at the smaller shops.

Retail Bespoke Tailoring

The Wages Council for this industry sets minimum weekly earnings at £51.40, but actual earnings vary tremendously with the type of establishment and the services provided. A custom tailor working in a fashionable area can earn £150.00 per week – even more if he does design work.

	£ Per Week
Assistant craftworkers	97–105.00
Craftworkers	110–115.00

The following jobs are common in each of these subgroups, as are the earnings.

	£ Per Week
General labourers	82.00
Porters and packers	82.00
Machinists and pressers	90.00
Machine and knife cutters	95.00
Measure cutters and tailors (precision work)	100–105.00

Hat, Cap and Millinery

The Wages Council for this industry sets out minimum weekly rates of £51.20. Earnings seem to be much the same for all production jobs, which include cutters, blockers, finishers, stretchers, and pressers. Earnings average around £90 per week, although piecework is common and can cause earnings to vary considerably.

LINEN FINISHERS

Many linen products require hand-finishing. The result is that much of the work can be done at home on piece rates. The linen industry is covered by a Wages Council order which sets a minimum level on earnings of £50 per week. Some workers can earn considerably more, especially those who can do custom embroidery and design work.

	£ per week
Machine operators	86.00
Embroidery machine operators	89.50
Samplemakers	98.00

LACE MAKERS

Lace makers are covered by a Wages Council order. Almost all workers in lace finishing are women — a great many do the jobs at home. Part-time work is very common, and the chance for overtime earnings is therefore reduced. Weekly earnings tend to be close to the Wages Council order, which is £44.40 per week.

OSTRICH AND FANCY FEATHER AND ARTIFICIAL FLOWER MAKERS

Yes, there is a Wages Council for Ostrich feather workers. The minimum weekly wage is £45. It was difficult to check on earnings, not being able to find anyone who actually did this for a living.

LAUNDRY WORKERS

There are two types of operations in the laundry industry; dry cleaning, which is a chemical process often done in large factories, and regular 'soap and water' cleaning. Most of the jobs are in the latter. The work tends to be heavy and hard, particularly in the smaller, less mechanised shops. Union membership is low, as are wages. The industry is covered by a Wages Council. The minimum rate is £51 per week but average earnings are £73 per week.

Piecework systems are common in laundering as are payment-by-results schemes. These payments, rather than overtime, are most likely to raise earnings. There is a shift premium of 1p per hour and a night work allowance of 20 per cent above the basic hourly rate.

CARPET MAKERS

About 30,000 workers are employed in the carpet industry, most of them in the West Midlands and in Yorkshire. The New Earnings Survey estimates that the average manual worker in the carpet industry earns £103 per week. Rates of pay for weavers will vary according to the width of the loom (wider looms are more difficult to operate).

	£ per week
Labourers	98.00
Material handlers	101.00
Weavers (single-cloth)	103.00
Weavers (double-cloth)	105.00
Jacquard weavers (loom that weaves figured fabrics)	
single-cloth	105.00
double-cloth	107.00

Fully 15 per cent of earnings comes from payment-by-result systems. Premium rates are paid for night work (an additional 34p per hour) and for those working consecutive shifts. The work week is guaranteed.

BRUSH AND BROOM MAKERS

Workers in brush and broom manufacture are essentially machine minders, although in some of the older firms, there is a considerable amount of hand-tying, etc. The minimum weekly rate of pay is £57.60. Average earnings are about 25 per cent above these rates.

CUTLERY AND SILVERWARE WORKERS

About 5,000 workers are employed in this industry which produces hollow ware (bowls, vessels, etc.) and flatwear (cutlery). Most firms are concentrated in and around the Sheffield area.

	£ per week
Craftsmen	125.00
Grade I workers	119.00
(skilled workers operating without supervision)	

	£ per week
Grade II workers (machine operators requiring some supervision)	117.00
Grade III (machine minders)	108.00
Grade IV (labourers)	90.00

About 20 per cent of earnings comes from overtime, shift, and payment-by-results schemes.

BUTTON MAKERS

Fewer than 1,000 workers are involved in button making, many of them homeworkers. Firms are quite small and are covered by a Wages Council order setting minimum weekly earnings at £46. Homeworkers are paid a minimum of 76p per hour. In practice, actual earnings are considerably higher – around £80 per week. Workers in the Pin, Hook, and Eye and Snap Fastener industry were covered by a separate Wages Council which set their minimum pay at £52.50 per week, but actual earnings seem to be about the same as for button maker. (The Wages Council was abolished this year.)

CERAMIC WORKERS

About 60,000 employees work in the pottery industry which has its centre in North Staffordshire. The New Earnings Survey estimates that the average manual worker in the ceramics industry earn £106 per week. Almost 20 per cent of that comes from payment-by-results systems.

	£ per week
Engravers	119.00
Modellers	115.00
Mouldmakers	113.00
Throwers	108.00

	£ per week
Hand shapers	105.00
Platemakerss	102.00
Labourers	98.00

Weekend overtime is paid at twice the basic rate.

POTTERS/CHINA WORKERS

	Day work	4 shifts
	£ per week	
Regular grade B (semi-skilled)	91.00	113.50
Higher Grade C (training required)	101.00	123.00
Special Grade D (individual responsibility high training)	106.60	128.00
All workers	106.10	

GLASS WORKERS

About 80,000 employees work in the glass industry, almost all of them process workers in large, mechanised plants. The following jobs are typical of those in glassware, flatglass and flatglass processing.

	£ per week
Sandblaster, Kiln Fitter	136.00
Cutter, Glazier, Silverer	129.00
Machine Operator	124.00
Windscreen Fitter	119.00
Sand Washer, Cleaner	115.00

CHEMICAL WORKERS

Chemical companies set their wages together through the Chemical Industries Association, but the largest employer, Imperial Chemical Industries Ltd., negotiates independently and tends to pay higher wages. Chemicals are a continuous production industry; because the plants do not shut down, workers must take on shifts that include night and weekend work. The nature of the shift, therefore, determines pay.

	£ Per Week
Day Workers	100.00
Continuous 3-Shift Workers	127.00
Non-continuous 3-Shift Workers	111.70
2-Shift Workers	111.75
Night Workers	114.90

Benefits: These figures include special shift premiums which at I.C.I. are:

	£ Per Week
3-Shift Continuous	23.61
3-Shift Non-continuous	11.64
2-Shift Non-continuous	8.25
Permanent Night Work	23.61

FILM DEVELOPERS
These rates are for workers in 'batch' or bulk film processing. In general, earnings are about 15 per cent above these rates.

	£ per week
Foremen	107.00
Section Supervisor	100.00
Emulsion Coater	91.00
Film Guillotinist	85.00
Coating Assistant	82.00

PRINTERS
1980 saw the collapse of the system by which a centrally-negotiated agreement between the print

unions and the employers was reached on wages thoughout the country. Agreements are now negotiated plant by plant. A typical book printer's average earnings for a 40-hour week are given below. They include basic pay, plus supplements, plus the average bonus. Overtime can raise these earnings above these rates.

More is paid for skilled work involved with film setting and preparation for litho printing.

	£ per week
National Graphical Association Craftsmen (typesetters, machine minders)	109.00
Society for Graphical and Allied Trades Class 1 (Bookbinders and any apprenticeship-trained job)	109.00
Class 2 (semi-skilled)	100.28
Class 3 (unskilled)	95.37

SUPERVISORS/FOREMEN

Supervisors are responsible for maintaining production and discipline. The continuous process industries (chemicals and petroleum) have the highest percentage of supervisors probably because the maintenance of production is so important. Pay varies according to responsibilities and by industry. Some of the main groups are set out below.

	£ Per Week
Chemical Processing	155.00
Food and Drink Processing	124.00
Electrical	150.00
Machine Maintenance	139.00
Metal Manufacture	136.00

	£ per week
Printing	133.00
Woodworking	118.50
Inspection and Assembly	131.50
Building	126.00

STOCKROOM WORKERS

In wholesale and retail operations:

	£ per week
Labourers	90.00
Supervisors	94.00
Managers — small operations	114.00
large operations	120.00

POST OFFICE WORKERS

The Post Office is divided into three industries: Telecommunications, Posts, and National Girobank. Together they employ over 425,000 workers represented by nine trade unions. The following rates and salaries do not include overtime, productivity or shift payments which can raise earnings about one third above these figures. The New Earnings Survey estimates that the average telephonist earns £104.00 per week and that postmen and mail sorters earn about £105.00.

	£ per week
Telephonists	40.82
at age 19	78.47
Adult recruits	73.25

	£ per week
Telegraphists	46.04
at age 19	88.51
Adult recruits	79.82
Overseas Telegraph operators	48.48
by age 19	91.60

	£ per week
Adult recruits	82.63
Postal assistants	45.26
by age 19	81.23
Adult recruits	79.82
Post Office Tower Attendants	74.51
Post Office Tower Security Wardens	82.63

	£ per year
Radio Officers	4,094
by age 25	5,209–6,860

The hours of work are 41 per week in London and 42 elsewhere. The London allowance is £1,081 per year in inner and £536 in outer London.

DOCKERS/STEVEDORES

Stevedores are labourers who load and unload ships. The New Earnings Survey estimates that the average stevedore earns £146.05 per week. £22.02 of that comes from overtime work, and £31.02 comes from payment-by-results schemes. The national wage contracts are substantially supplemented at separate negotiations in each port.

AIR TRANSPORT WORKERS

The New Earnings Survey estimates that the average manual worker in air transport earns £143.70 per week. About 10 per cent of that comes as shift pay and another 10 per cent as overtime. The following are the maximum basic rates (not earnings) in air transport.

Ground Services Staff	£ per week
Lowest grades	84.37
Highest grade	116.85

Maintenance Grades	£ per week
Lead tradesmen	127.82
Tradesmen	110.34
Senior production assistants	118.77
Production assistants	110.34
Group maintenance leader	104.55
Aircraft component worker	99.31

Actual earnings would average about 30 per cent above these rates.
The London allowance is £15.67 per week for inner and £6.62 per week for outer London.

VEHICLE CONSTRUCTION

The New Earnings Survey estimates that the average manual worker employed in motor vehicle manufacture earns just over £117 per week; those making agricultural vehicles earn about £119 per week. About 25 per cent of earnings in both cases are output-related (overtime, shift and payments-by-result). The following figures are the basic rates for motor vehicle manufacture in Ford and British Leyland — two firms one hears a great deal about. These figures include a weekly attendance bonus.

	Ford	British Leyland
	£ per week	
Washers, Polishers	94.60	72.40
Assembler, Welding Machine Operators	103.50	77.80
Paint Sprayers, Upholters, Metal Finishers	108.00	89.35
Tool Estimators	112.90	98.00
Toolmakers, Specialist Sheet Metal Workers	121.00	105.50

The working week is 40 hours and there is guaranteed employment for most hourly employees. The London allowance is 0.21p per hour.

MOTOR VEHICLE MECHANICS

The Motor Vehicle repair industry consists of a large number of operations, each employing relatively few workers. Union membership is relatively low. The New Earnings Survey estimates that the average mechanic earns £108 per week while those with less skill average £99.50.

	£ per week
Apprentices	44.00 − 83.50 (rises with age)
Operatives working outside the shop	
Petrol Pump, etc.	65.00
Operatives in the workshop	76.00
Semi-skilled	84.00
Skilled	108.00
Technicians	110.00
Foremen	121.50

Mechanics have a very complicated premium schedule for extra shift work. Night shift workers scheduled to work any combination of five days receive a quarter premium on all hours worked. Work undertaken on a sixth day earns an additional 50 per cent premium on top of the quarter increase; work on a seventh day earns a 100 per cent premium, again in addition to the quarter increase.

MAINTENANCE CRAFTSMEN

Maintenance craftsmen repair and maintain industrial equipment. Their skills are those of traditional craftsmen: carpentry, painting, plumbing, etc., but they work in highly mechanised industries. As a result they work separately from the main labour force and have higher status and pay. What makes them stand out is not that they earn more than similarly skilled workers elsewhere, but that they earn more than other employees in the organisation. In practice, employers have one 'craft rate' that applies to all these craftsmen. As a group, however, they have considerable bargaining power within a plant.

	£ per week
Maintenance Carpenters	106.00
Non-electrical Maintenance Fitters	128.70
Motor Mechanics	108.20
Maintenance Foremen (electric)	150.00
Maintenance Electricians (in plants)	133.60
Maintenance Electricians (on ships)	127.40
Mechanical and Electrical Maintenance Fitters	117.10
Maintenance Pipefitters	111.80

POWER ENGINEERS/ELECTRICAL SUPPLY

These engineers control the production and distribution of electricity. They are employed by the national electricity industry.

	£ Per Year
Electrical control grades (technicians)	5,395–5,925
Engineers (lowest grade)	5,925–8,965
(highest grade)	9,215–12,805
Senior Engineers	10,905–14,070
Principal Engineers	13,645–15,815

Because the demand for electricity varies considerably, the possibility of work outside normal hours is very great. There are special allowances for shift work outside normal hours which can be as much as £2,800 per year for the highest grade of engineers. Premium payments for temporary work outside normal hours can be as much as £27.50 per hour. In addition, there is a bonus for extra responsibility of £246 per year. The London allowance is £765 for inner and £440 for outer London.

ATOMIC ENERGY WORKERS

There are two employers in the nuclear energy industry: the Atomic Energy Authority (public sector) and British Nuclear Fuels (private sector).

Although the work appears to be about the same in both, pay is higher in the latter. The nature of these jobs is routine — much like maintenance employees in engineering. The conditions under which they are performed are different.

	£ Per Week
General Workers	86.90 – 109.00
Craftsmen	114.00 – 129.00

Perks: Irksome clothing allowance of 9p to 40p for time spent in impervious clothing. Additional allowances are paid for abnormal conditions.

CHAPTER EIGHT

Others

ROYAL FAMILY

Income from the Civil List is not in fact 'pay' but an allowance made by the State to the Sovereign and the Royal satellites to cover the cost of expenses incurred by them in the performance of their public duties. Three-quarters of the Queen's Civil List goes toward staff wages (there are, for example, 350 employees at Buckingham Palace). In addition to the list, Prince Charles receives about £400,000 from the Duchy of Cornwall; the Queen receives an additional £700,000 from the Duchy of Lancaster. An allowance of £274,000 is divided between the Dukes of Gloucester and Kent and Princess Alexandra. Currently, Prince Andrew takes only one-quarter of his entitlement listed below.

	£ per year
The Queen's Civil List	3,260,200
Queen Elizabeth the Queen Mother	286,000
The Duke of Edinburgh	160,000
Princess Anne	100,000
Prince Andrew	20,000
Princess Margaret	98,000

	£ per year
Princess Alice Duchess of Gloucester	40,000
The Duke of Gloucester	78,000
The Duke of Kent	106.000
Princess Alexandra	101,000
Total	4,249,273
Refunded by the Queen	285,073
	3,964,200

Perks: Nice places to stay — Buckingham Palace, Windsor Castle, Holyrood House, Kensington Palace, St. James's Palace, Balmoral, Sandringham, Gatcombe, and Highgrove House. The State contributes £5,699,912 for their upkeep. Royal Travel — from the Royal Yacht to the Royal Train, the State contributes £11,635,000 for running costs and upkeep.
The Queen pays no tax on the Civil List.

SECURITY/PROTECTION EMPLOYEES
These workers are employed by private companies to provide security for goods or for people. Security workers are employed directly by companies (such as night watchmen) and by specialised protection firms. The market for these specialised services is very competitive. Recruitment has traditionally been from the police and armed forces, but that nexus has been weakened in recent years as pay in the armed services and the police increased. The one outstanding characteristic of this work is that hours tend to be extremely long; working weeks of 50 and 60 hours are not uncommon. The New Earnings Survey estimates that security patrolmen earn on average £115 per week — £22.50 of that from overtime pay. Security officers earn £119.00 per week — £21.50 of that from overtime.

Security Officer/Watchman
Part of a plant's staff. Responsible for the
security of keys, registers visitors, checks
doors after closing, etc. Earnings vary between
£80 and £95 per week depending on responsibilities. A fair proportion of that pay comes from
overtime and night-shift premiums.

Store Detectives
These employees wander the shop floor to watch
for pilfering. This work is increasingly
sub-contracted to private agencies. Basic rates
are higher than for security officers, but
earnings are not much different because
night-shift premiums are generally not relevant
here. They earn £95 per week.

Hotel Detectives
Protect hotel property and its guests. Responsibilities and earnings will vary depending on
the size of the hotel. Large hotels will pay an
annual salary of £6,000 – 7,000.

The following figures are for workers in private
security agencies.

	£ per week	Hours overtime
Cash-in-transit Leaders	110.00	14
Static Sergeants	113.00	20
Beats Sergeant (on patrol)	117.00	18
Section Inspectors	140.00	22

PRIVATE INVESTIGATORS
Private investigators are paid by the case, so
their earnings will vary depending on the nature
and amount of work that they do. They usually
charge clients a flat hourly rate of about

£20. Clients also pay any of the investigator's expenses while on the job – such as transportation and accommodation. The investigatory staff earn between £4,500 and £7,000 per year in the provinces and between £5,000 and £8,000 in London along with the use of a car.

COMPUTING WORKERS

The computer has invaded every industry, and the demand for data processing skills is high. Salaries have risen dramatically in the past year, even for those with limited experience. The figures below are for computing jobs in the Greater London area.

Operators run the actual equipment and are not generally involved with programming work. They are likely to work irregular shifts which include unsocial hours.

	£ per year
Computer Operators	4,250 – 4,750
Senior Operators	6,250 – 6,750
(2-5 years experience)	
Operations/Shift Managers	9,000 – 11,000

Programmers organise the data and construct the software to process it.

	£ per year
Programmers	4,400 – 4,600
Senior Programmers	6,600 – 7,500
Junior Analysts	7,000 – 8,500
Senior Analysts	7,500 – 10,000
Technical Managers/Data Processing Manager	9,800 – 13,000

Board members of computer companies are rather better paid. T.C. Hudson, Chairman of International Computers Ltd., had a salary of

£45,000 in 1980 while the highest paid director of the firm, presumably Dr. C.M. Wilson the managing director, was paid £77,000.

KEY PUNCH OPERATORS
Operate key punching machines to record data on cards for use by computers. When employed for a 40-hour week, they earn about £85. Freelance workers charge by the key impression or at an hourly rate of about £1.75 plus machine rental or user fees.

UNIVERSITY TECHNICIANS
Technicians are employed almost entirely in the laboratories of the physical sciences. These salaries were based on an award from the Clegg Commission.

	£ Per Year
Department Supervisor	8,481-10,785
Laboratory Supervisor	7,600-8,542
Animal Laboratory Worker	5,284-6,078
Laboratory Technician	4,672-5,473
Animal House Worker	4,228-4,801

METALLURGISTS
Study and offer advice on the extraction, processing, and use of metals and alloys. A very high proportion of metallurgists are in the engineering industry. The New Earnings Survey estimates that the average metallurgist earns about £151 per week, up 31 per cent from 1979. The data below are based on a survey now about a year old. They have been adjusted by this rate of increase to more accurately approximate earnings. This estimate, then, is a very crude one.

	Workers Age 35-39
	£ per year
Technical Administration	8,250
Production	8,970

	£ per year
Research and Development	8,450
Teaching	9,620
All Metallurgists	7,600

PHYSICISTS

Study matter and energy and their interaction. Their research can be very abstract or very practical. Most are employed to do the latter. The fields of acoustics, optics, and mechanics, for example, can be extremely useful to industry. The following figures are total earnings from employment for physicists by employer. Because the age distributions across employers are very different (physicists in consulting firms, for example, seem to be on average very young), it may be misleading to quote average earnings. Instead, median earnings are presented for those aged 35 to 39.

	£ Per Year
Central government	9,300
Health authority	10,550
Public corporations	10,150
United Kingdom Atomic Authority	9,330
Industry	9,010
University	9,250

Virtually everyone in these positions has a graduate degree.

CHEMISTS

Study the properties of substances and the transformations that they undergo. The differences between chemists and chemical engineers is somewhat tenuous and seems to centre on the immediate applicability of research, the latter being more practical. The following figures are median earnings for Fellows and

members of the Royal Institute of Chemistry – all
of whom have university degrees.

	£ Per Year
Central government	10,000
Area Health Authority	9,230
University	10,770
Industry or Commerce	9,600

PHARMACISTS

Retail pharmacy is an interesting mix of public
and private sector influence. The National Health
Service negotiataes a contract with retail
pharmacies whereby the latter agree to dispense
drugs and the NHS agrees to make a contribution
to the non-retail costs of operating the
pharmacy. In chain stores, where pharmacies are
run by Pharmacist Managers (as opposed to
proprietors), the contract also sets out salaries
for them which vary with the shop's turnover.
Scales for pharmacists do not vary with
turnover. In each case, these rates are minimums
which are often exceeded.

Pharmacist Managers Weekly turnover	London £ per year	Provinces £ per year
£1,380 to £1,517	5,776	5,698
£1,518 to £1,669	5,892	5,812
£1,670 to £1,836	6,009	5,928
£1,837 to £2,019	6,130	6,047
£2,020 to £2,222	6,253	6,168
£2,223 to £2,444	6,377	6,291
£2,445 to £2,688	6,505	6,417
£2,689 to £2,957	6,635	6,545
£2,958 to £3,253	6,767	6,676
£3,254 to £3,578	6,902	6,809
£3,579 and over	7,040	6,945

Pharmacists	£ per year	£ per year
1st year after registration	4,278	4,202
2nd year after registration	4,429	4,353

Pharmacists do not earn overtime for rota work performed as part of the employer's contract with the NHS. When such work is performed on Sundays, short days, and customary holidays, the rate of pay is £4.50 per hour.

The following are minimum rates for dispensing assistants and shop assistants. Shop assistants will actually earn around £90 in the London area while Dispensing Assistants earn about £100.

Dispensing Assistants	London £ per week	Provinces £ per week
Age 20	61.60	61.21
21	63.30	62.90

Shop Assistants

Provinces 'A' have a population of over 10,000

	London	Provinces 'A'	Provinces 'B'
Age 16	36.70	36.40	36.15
17	42.30	42.00	41.75
18	47.90	47.60	47.35
19	50.70	50.40	50.15
20	56.30	56.00	55.75

Pharmacists employed by Health Authorities.

	£ per year
Basic Grade Pharmacist	5,470 − 6,889
Staff Pharmacist	7,610 − 10,152
Principal Pharmacist	10,352 − 13,955
Principal Pharmacist (highest grade)	14,175 − 15,536
Area Pharmaceutical Officers	14,402 − 15,763
Regional Pharmaceutical Officers	15,989 − 17,350

SHOP ASSISTANTS
Retail Trade

The retail industry is one of Britain's largest industries, employing over 2 million workers in almost 400,000 outlets. There are two Wages Councils in retailing – Food and Non-food Trades, which together cover about half the total work force. Shops are catergorised as multiples, co-operatives, and independents coinciding roughly with the size of operations. There has been a trend in recent years towards multiples, and stores have been getting larger (witness the growth of 'supermarket' into 'hypermarket'). But the independents still account for about half of all retail trade. The vast majority of outlets have only a handful of employees, and they are unlikely to be union members. Wages are low in retailing, often close to the Wages Council orders. It may be because much of the work is part-time and low-skilled. The New Earnings Survey estimates that shop assistants, shelf-fillers and other retail workers as a group earn an average of £90 per week.

Wages Council Orders (Minimum Rates)	£ per week
Retail Trades (non-food)	52.00
Bookselling and Stationery	52.00
Retail Drapery, Outfitting and Footwear	52.10
Retail Furnishing	52.00
Retail Food	51.50

The following rates are common for jobs in retail food:

	£ per week
Checkout Clerks	60.00
Stockists	68.00
Night Stockists	82.00

	£ per week
Delicatessan/Off-Licence	
Clerks or Assistants	60.50
Produce Workers	65.00
Fishmongers	65.00
Butcher's Cutters	68.00

Non-Food Retail	£ per week
Sales Assistants	60.00
Sales Clerks	62.00
Display Assistants	65.00
Display Clerks	69.00
Department Supervisor	75.00

Overtime and other output-related payments can raise earnings to levels significantly above these rates. This is particularly true for non-food retail workers who are usually salesworkers paid partly through commissions. These extra payments alone can raise earnings 25 per cent or more above the basic rates. Actual earnings will average 30-40 per cent above these rates.

Managers

Store managers and assistant store managers are not particularly well-paid. Their salaries tend to rise with the size of their stores. Assistant managers in small shops are only marginally better paid than their employees. In large stores (weekly trade over £20,000), they can earn about £125 per week. Shop or store managers in these operations can earn about £175. Of course, bonus schemes can add to their income. Retailing is however better paid in the higher echelons. Many firms such as Moss Bros and Liberty of Regent Street are still privately controlled. Here the salaries of top executives are less generous than those of the larger groups. B.H. Moss, chairman of Moss Bros was paid £15,504 in 1979 while their highest paid director received £22,751. Sir Hugh Fraser, until earlier this year chairman of the firm his father founded, House of Fraser, had in 1980 a salary of £21,000 to augment his substantial shareholding while their highest paid director, presumably managing director Mr. W.G. Crossan, received £53,000. Debenhams paid the Chairman, Sir Anthony Burney, £30,550 in that same year while the highest paid director had a salary of £55,684.

WINDOW DRESSERS

Window dressing is considered part of a store's advertising and is co-ordinated with the general advertising programme. The manager of the window dressing group or section is responsible for designing and producing all the displays in the shop, usually around different themes. The manager is paid the same general salary as department heads: about £9,000 per year in larger department stores.

HAIRDRESSING

About 100,000 employees work in the hair-dressing industry. There is virtually no trade union representation or collective bargaining. The Hairdressing Wages Council has established the minimum weekly wage for the industry at £36 per week.

	£ per week	
	In Provinces	In London
Shampooists	60.00	65.00
Manicurists/cashiers	71.05	75.00
Hairdressers	75.00	79.00
after 2 years	84.00	88.00
Charge hands	89.00	91.00
Shop Managers	107.00	120.00

Most shops are small so that many have no manicurists, for example, and the duties of the manager are often combined with a hairdresser's – especially where the owner works in the shop. Tips cause earnings to vary, especially in the more expensive London shops.

MODELS

Models serve as patterns for painters, sculptors or photographers. They also display garments and accessories. The former are known as artist's models, and their employment is often on a very casual basis. Models for artists or sculptors are generally paid by the sitting, which works out at about £2 per hour. Photographic models can be highly paid; one difference here is that the model's image and identity are clearly recognisable and much more important to the outcome than in paintings or sculpture. Models with a well-known image or a following can command several hundred pounds for a magazine's cover photo. The range in fees is enormous, however, between models and between magazines, but the standard fee is around £150 per session.

Fashion models display clothing and accessories. Their compensation depends almost entirely on where they model. Fashion shows in provincial contres can pay local models £10 – 20 per show, but these models are essentially amateurs who work part time. Major fashion shows in London cater to an international market, and the market for models who work these shows is also international. Models working a very big show would receive about £200 as well as all their expenses – including airfares to the show. Top fashion models based in New York City (which seems to be the centre for fashion models) can earn £30 – 40,000 per year.

Top photographic models can also command large
daily rates. While an inexperienced, but up and
coming model will earn only about £100 per day at
the peak of her career she can expect to earn
£2,000 for an eight hour session. All expenses
are on top.

Babies receive a fee of £50 per advertisement
with a further £50 if it is used.

AIRLINE PERSONNEL

About 75,000 people work for airlines in Britain,
75 per cent of them for British Airways. Other
British airlines are required by the Civil
Aviation Act of 1949 to employ their workers on
conditions at least equal to those for comparable
jobs in British Airways. Because there are a
large number of airlines with operations in
Britain, the market for airline personnel –
particularly in-flight crew – becomes in some
sense international, and the rates that apply in
Britain reasonably approximate those in the rest
of the world. The composition of the cockpit crew
varies with the type of plane, but the following
positions are representataive of those in the
industry.

Pilot-in-Command

This is the senior position in the flight crew.
He is qualified and responsible for every aspect
of the flight.

Co-Pilot

There are sometimes two co-pilots whose duties
include navigation and monitoring of the plane's
systems as well as providing back-up personnel.

Flight Engineer

This position is filled by an engineer – albeit
one qualified as a pilot. His duties are limited

to monitoring the plane's equipment. A flight engineer is not present in every plane; in many planes, his duties are taken by the co-pilot.

Entry-level pay for a co-pilot starts at £6,600 per year. It rises to £22,000 for senior pilots-in-command. Flight Engineers are paid on a co-pilot's scale. Many pilots enter airlines with experience from the armed services. In these circumstances they would start at a reasonably high level.

Cabin Crew

The stewards and stewardesses in the cabin are responsible for the passengers and their safety during the flight. Their pay ranges from the basic entry-level rate of £3,900 per year to £9,500 for senior supervisors.

Flight crews obviously get sent all around the world. They are responsible for their own accommodation once they land. Airlines provide a form of shift pay – payments that vary with the destination of the flight – to compensate for these expenses on the ground. Payments for long flights to expensive cities are greater than others. Work schedules in the airline industry get shifted a great deal, and combinations of work time and leave do not always follow a regular pattern. On European flights, however, the general arrangement is three days off for every six days of flying.

Perks: After one year's service, personnel are allowed a 90 per cent reduction on regular airfares on any flight where space is available. Some airlines extend this perk to members of the employee's immediate family. And some airlines have reciprocal arrangements whereby their employees get similar discount rates on other airlines.

AIRPORT FUEL TRUCK DRIVERS

The following basic rates are for drivers of tanker trucks at Heathrow Airport. Actual earnings will average about 25 per cent above these figures. Drivers work a six-day schedule.

	£ per week
Senior Drivers	124.00
Drivers	120.00

The London Allowance is £727 per year for inner and £356 for outer London.

CHAUFFEURS

Are paid differently according to the terms of their employment. Those hired for a fixed work schedule or available during fixed times typically earn about £95 per week. They might be employed by a firm to drive the Director to work or by a private firm which hires limousine service to the well-heeled. Earnings can increase rapidly where premium payments are made for overtime work and for work outside normal hours. It is still common for chauffeurs to be employed as part of a domestic staff; they would live on or nearby the premises of the employer and be available for service almost any time. Earnings would be significantly lower – about £45 – but board and lodging would be provided.

TAXI DRIVERS

The taxi business can be divided into three parts. Owner-drivers own their cars, pay their own expenses, and take their income as net receipts. Journeymen rent cars from a cab company and pay a flat fee plus some percentage of their gross receipts. Journeymen usually pay for their own petrol. Employees of cab companies are paid a low minimum hourly rate and some percentage of their gross receipts. In all cases tips go directly to the drivers. In London and most other provincial centres, cabs and drivers must be licensed and fares are set by legislation. Conditions of employment and minimum commissions for employees are set by negotiation. Outside London, licensing and fare regulations are less common; most drivers are owners who work part-time. How much one earns, therefore, depends on what type of driver one is, where one works, one's hours and luck in getting good tips and fares. There are 12,600 licensed taxis in London – 7,500 of these are run by owner/drivers. Non-owners receive one-third of the meter fare plus tips. They pay between £60 to £85 per week to hire the taxi. On a good evening, taxi drivers can take in £100. Weekly earnings, after expenses, might average £140, but the variation is tremendous.

BUS DRIVERS AND CONDUCTORS

The following rates are paid to conductors and drivers employed on buses operated by London Transport. Because of overtime, shiftwork, etc., actual earnings will average 35–40 per cent above these rates.

	£ Per Week
On two-man buses:	
Conductors	78.67
Drivers	67.22
One-man buses:	
Drivers	92.32

Drivers on one-man buses receive a supplement of 15p per hour on routes that are especially difficult and busy. A bonus of £50.00 per year is paid to all workers with more than 12 months service. The London allowance is £8.71 per week which is payable to almost everyone.

RAILWAYMEN

Although there is some private rail service in Britain, most trains are operated by the government through British Rail. Because trains operate at all hours, the amount of shift work and overtime hours is substantial – accounting for over one-third of earnings. The average manual worker in British Rail makes about £108 per week.

	£ per week
Locomotive drivers, Motormen	115.00
Signalmen, Shuntmen	114.00
Track machinemen, Trackmen	116.00
Officemen and Driver's Relief Assistants	105.00

Premium rates are paid for nightwork, Saturday and Sunday work, and unsocial hours. Additional payments are made to workers who travel more than 200 miles during their shift. The London allowance is £8.50 per week.

METRO WORKERS

The following rates are for workers on the Tyne-Wear Metro in Newcastle.

	£ Per Week
Supervisor	133.00
Station controller	127.00
	£ per week
Trainman	88.00
Overhead linesmen	75.00
Tunnel cleaner	73.00
Labourer	71.00

Productivity bonuses can be as much as 30 per cent of basic rates for certain practices and additional responsibilities.

SHIP MASTERS

The duties of ships, personnel vary tremendously
with the size of the ship. Home-trade ships,
those which ply the coastal regions of Britain,
have small crews whose jobs are relatively
simple. Foreign-going ships have larger crews
whose responsibilities are much greater. The
Master of a foreign-going ship, say an oil
tanker, is responsible for every aspect of the
voyage. He will earn between £13 and 14,000 per
year with a minimum of 120 leave days each year
(the average is around 130). These rates vary,
however, from company to company depending on the
type of voyage. The New Earnings Survey estimates
that average earnings for all ships' officers is
£178 per week. The average earnings for deck and
engineroom hands is £134 per week. Earnings on
large, foreign-going ships would be closer to
£150.

MERCHANT NAVY/SEA TRANSPORT

The New Earnings Survey estimates that the
average manual worker in sea transport earns
£138.80 per week, a substantial component of
which comes from overtime work about £31. Given
the nature of shipping and the fact that one is
'at work' the entire length of the voyage, it is
not surprising that hours extend beyond the
normal 40. The following figures are basic rates
in the Merchant Navy. Actual earnings will
average about 30 per cent above these rates.

Rating	Weekly national standard rates £
Deck Department:	
Carpenters	65.55 - 82.25
Chief Petty Officers	69.75 - 79.85
Petty Officers	67.65

Rating	Weekly national standard rates
	£
Seamen	58.50 - 64.00
Engine-Room Department:	
Plumbers	72.12 - 82.25
Senior Mechanics	71.52 - 81.65
Chief Petty Officers	69.75 - 79.85
Petty Officers	67.65
Motormen	58.50 - 64.00
Stewards' Department:	
Chief Steward	79.85 - 89.95
Second steward	64.00
Steward	61.57
Galley Department:	
Chief Cooks/Cook Stewards	68.75 - 79.85
Second Cooks	65.55
Assistant Cooks	62.27

WATERWAYS STAFF

	£ per year
Building Inspectors	6,079-6,557
Workshop Managers	6,852-7,631
Repairyard Managers	8,503-9,154
Senior Assistant Engineer	10,276-11,022
Dock Manager/Water Engineer	11,497-12,420

DIVERS

Work under water usually in construction or ship repair. Divers must be familiar not just with specialised air supply equipment, but also with construction and repair tools specifically designed for underwater work. They often have a variety of technical skills in addition to those simply related to diving.

River divers are employed largely by water authorities and work in reservoirs, canals and rivers installing and repairing equipment. They usually operate in teams of three or more. Overtime accounts for more than one third of total earnings; premium payments (twice basic hourly rates for time spent in underwater work) can account fore another 20 per cent.

The senior diver in a river diving team receives basic pay of about £85 for a 39 hour week. Average overtime payments would be about £36 per week and bonus of £25 per week would also be received. Total earnings, assuming an average diving time of about 10 hours per week, would be just under £170 per week. The bottom position on the team is the linesman who is responsible for the equipment and rarely dives himself. His weekly earnings are substantially less, about £120 per week, because he does not earn the diving premium rates.

Deep sea or ocean divers earn subtantially more than river divers; the work is much more dangerous and their skills often include sophisticated underwater construction techniques. These divers often establish their own companies and subcontract work on oil rigs, etc. They also receive premium rates for time spent underwater. Annual earnings are between £20 and £30,000 for those with their own diving companies or those working for them, but a large amount of travelling is required and expenses can be considerable.

OIL-RIG WORKERS
Construction
It is easy to see that conditions on an oil-rig could be very harsh. Conditions on a half-built rig could only be worse. As a result, the pay for oil-rig construction workers should be quite high to compensate for the hardship. When on the

construction site, employees work almost a seven-day week and 10 - 12 hours a day. They continue at that pace for about 30 days and then receive a week of holiday on shore. Overtime is paid on the basis of a 40-hour week: that often means 30 or more hours of overtime pay (1½ premium) each week. Leave pay is accumulated at the rate of about 50-75p per working hour. When all bonuses and productivity payments are included, skilled craftsmen can earn over £14,000 per annum for a 40-week year. The following are hourly rates before overtime.

	£ per hour
Labourers	3.50
Semi-skilled workers	3.75
Craftsmen	4.20

GAS TECHNICIANS

These employees are responsible for the distribution of natural and town gas. The distribution networks are complex and not necessarily standardised from place to place. Like electricity, the demand for gas often varies by time and location, which makes its distribution a difficult task. The skills required tend to be those of the engineer.

	£ per year
General service (clerical work)	3,603-4,234
Highest grade (general service)	7,160-8,135
Senior officers	7,700-8,863
Senior officers (highest grade)	9,140-10,530

The London allowance is £751 per year for inner London, £415 for outer, and £154 for the fringe of London.

SURVEYORS

When the building industry suffers, so do surveyors. A great number of surveyors are self-employed, charging a fee for each job performed. The need for surveyors declines as construction falls off, which is the case this year.

	£ per year
Self-employed surveyors (private firms)	12,000–16,000
Teachers of surveying	11,100
Employed by construction firms	8,200
Department heads in construction firms	9,950

There is a growing demand for surveyors overseas, however, in areas where massive construction is taking place. The following salaries are for relative juniors:*

	£ per year
Australia	10,250
Hong Kong	10,500
Kenya	10,530
Kuwait	20,000
Oman	11,692
Saudi Arabia	13,000
South Africa	11,136

* Building 23 January 1981, p. 107.

Other positions in the construction industry:

	£ per year
Purchasing managers	6,400–8,000
Estimate assessors	7,500–10,300
Contract/Subcontract Managers	9,400–12,800

VERIFIER/INSPECTOR

Ensures accuracy of reports and assesses products and services, mainly for consumer guides. Duties include travelling to hotels and restaurants as well as testing consumer products such as cars and televisions. Earnings for full-time workers average about £6,500, but a great deal of the work is done by freelance, part-time staff. All expenses are usually paid. Often the only compensation for part-time workers is some help with expenses – particularly where reports are on travel facilities.

AUTOMOBILE CLUB STAFF

	£ per year
Breakdown Information	3,700 – 4,100
Patrol Force	4,000 – 7,700
Hotel Inspectors	3,500 – 4,900

Perks: Hotel inspectors have all their food and living expenses paid when on the job.

MESSENGERS

Collect and deliver items within and between offices. Those working outside an office must have good knowledge of the local geography. The method of transport – car, motorcycle, bicycle, or public transport – is either provided by the employer or the messenger's costs are reimbursed. Companies either employ their own messengers or subcontract the work to private delivery agencies.

	£ per year
In-house Messengers	3,400 – 3,600
Private Agency Bicycle Messengers	3,600 – 4,200
Motorcycle Messengers (requires licence)	3,800 – 4,300
Dispatcher/Supervisor	4,500

Shift and overtime pay contributes significantly to earnings. Weekend and holiday work, for example, is common.

STUDENTS

British students undertaking certain kinds of further education are eligible for maintenance grants from the government. Mandatory grants are those which local educational authorities must pay to students attending most full-time courses – such as university first degree or education diploma courses. Discretionary awards are made by local educational authorities for course work not covered by the mandatory system. Each authority decides for itself which of these courses to sponsor. The maintenance grant covers the period during terms as well as Easter and Christmas holidays. Students may claim supplementary benefits during the long summer vacation if they are unable to find a job. The grant is usually paid directly to the college or university, along with tuition and other fees. The following are the basic maintenance grants paid by local educational authorities.

	£ per year
Students attending courses in the London area	1,695
Students attending courses outside the London area	1,430
Students living in the parental home	1,125
Students who receive free board and lodging (other than at home)	595

Additional grants are made when required attendance exceeds the normal academic year (as in some special courses), for necessary travel, and for special equipment.

Deductions from the grant are made when the student's income exceeds £310 per year. The most important deductions, however, are those based on parental income. While there are a great number of exceptions and qualifications, the basic relationship is set out below.

Parental Income £ per year	Contribution £
Below 5,800	0
5,800	20
5,900	34
6,000	48
7,000	191
8,000	321
9,000	446
10,000	571
12,000	801
14,000	955
16,000	1,109
18,000+	1,263

The minimum maintenance payment made by the government is £385 per year. In addition to these government grants, students can receive scholarships and exhibition awards from their colleges and universities. These pay between £50 and £200 per year – more of an honour than a financial windfall.

It should be pointed out that parents can give their children up to £3,000 without incurring capital transfer tax, but few students will be able to match Cecil Rhodes who supported himself on an income of £3,000 per annum while an undergraduate at Oxford in 1873. Such a sum would be equivalent to £25,000 in 1981.

Post-graduates also receive grants which vary slightly in size according to which government agency gives them; social sciences are administered separately from physical sciences, for example. The grants are around £2,100 per year. In addition, the grant-giving body will pay for most reasonable research expenses which may include items such as foreign travel. These grants have no income-related deductions. It is interesting to note that Rhodes, Marshall, and Fulbright scholars from abroad receive a grant of approximately £3,000 per year, while they are students in the U.K.

SCHOOL CROSSING ATTENDANTS
The 'Lollipop' man or woman is nearly always a part-timer and often a pensioner but there is a minimum hourly rate of £1.47. The number of hours worked in any one year is of course restricted by school terms and the fact that you are only needed at the beginning and end of the the school day.

NEWSAGENTS
The Wages Council for Retail Food and Allied Trades sets the minimum weekly wage for Newsagent employees at £52.30. Actual earnings are around £80-90 per week.

EXHIBITION CRAFTSMEN
The exhibition industry produces signs and displays for advertising and industry. As the normal working week is only 38 hours, overtime and overtime pay are significant factors here. Overtime and other additional payments will raise earnings about 20 per cent over the basic rates, which are listed below.

	£ per week
Labourers	96.90
Craftsmen	107.54
Signwriters	110.75
Productions Artists	112.90

Workers in this industry frequently provide their own tools for which employers contribute a weekly allowance for £1.70 for carpenters and 85p for painters.

COUNSELLORS

Here we are referring to various types of social and personal conselling. How counsellors are paid and how much they earn depends on the type of counselling that they do - which in turn determines who employs them. (see Social Workers).

Marriage counsellors - are often members of the clergy who take on these jobs as part of their regular duties. Otherwise, the counsellors are volunteers.

Career counsellors - employed by schools and universities are paid according to teacher and lecturer rates, respectively.

Youth counsellors - are sometimes paid a small salary, usually about the level of lower clerical grades.

Most counselling is done part time as one part of a job's responsibilities or as volunteer work. Private counsellors charge clients between £10 and to £20 per hour.

FUNERAL WORKERS

	£ per year
Branch Manager	75.60
Assistant	75.60
Coffinmaker/polisher	72.00
Coffin finisher/bearer	63.00

Earnings are supplemented by a series of bonuses;
£5 per week for attendance, £3 per week for
agreeing to lunchtime work, and £4 per week for
agreeing to work during unsocial hours. These
bonuses are paid to all workers whether or not
lunchtime or unsocial hours work is performed.
Branch managers get a commission of 2.5 per cent
of gross receipts up to £60,000; 1.5 per cent of
the gross receipts over £60,000.

EMBALMERS

Undertakers arrange and manage funerals;
embalmers prepare the bodies. In most cases, the
two jobs are combined. Those who just prepare
bodies earn about £85 per week in the provinces
and £100 in London. Freelance work pays £6 per
body.

The cost to the client for embalming is £21, a
coffin will be a minimum of £100 while cremation
costs £50.

COFFIN AND CEREMENT MAKERS

The Wages Council for this industry has
established a minimum weekly rate of pay at
£46.40. Coffin-makers employ a number of skilled
workmen - particularly woodworkers - who make
around £100 per week.

CHAPTER NINE

Hours

The amount of time one spends at work is significant in its own right, but for those employees paid by the hour it has additional importance; hours worked determine earnings. Negotiations over the length of the work week are especially important because they determine the point at which premium overtime rates apply. Given this, attempts by work groups to shorten the working week may not be so much a desire for more leisure time as a desire for higher earnings by expanding the amount of work paid at overtime rates. In engineering, for example, the standard working week declined from 58½ hours in 1850 to 40 hours in 1980 (scheduled to fall to 39 in 1981), the greatest reductions coming at the turn of the century and immediately after the Second World War. Since the mid-1960's however, the standard work week has remained more or less the same (about 40 hours for male manual employees).

But this does not mean that the actual hours worked have declined by the same proportion. The New Earnings Survey indicates that the average manual worker actually puts in a 45.4-hour week, 5.4 hours over the average standard work week of 40. Those additional hours are paid at overtime rates and account for over 14 per cent of total earnings. Some 54 per cent of manual men put in overtime hours every week, and for these workers, total weekly hours average over 50.

It has been argued that employers have a financial incentive to extend overtime work rather than hire more employees because the costs of recruitment and training new workers often exceeds the cost of the overtime premium (usually one and a half the regular hourly rates). Trade unions have recently expressed a desire to restrict total hours of work – including overtime – perhaps as a means of protecting jobs. A great many agreements still specify a guaranteed amount of overtime, however, in addition to the standard work week.

It is striking to see just how much longer a manual worker's week is, although it is possible that a great deal of non-manual overtime never gets counted (work taken home, done on the train, etc.).

Average Hours Worked Per Week in 1980*

Manual Workers	Men	Overtime	Women	Overtime
All industries and services	45.4	5.7	39.6	1.1
All production industries	45.1	5.3	39.8	0.9
All manufacturing industries	45.0	5.2	39.8	0.9
All non-manufacturing industries	45.8	6.1	39.3	1.4
Non-Manual Workers				
All industries and services	38.7	1.6	36.7	0.4
All production industries	39.4	1.5	37.3	0.4

Non-Manual Workers	Men	Overtime	Women	Overtime
All manufacturing industries	39.4	1.6	37.3	0.5
All non-manufact- uring industries	38.5	1.6	36.6	0.4

* Source: New Earnings Survey 1980

Overtime Earnings as a % of Total Earnings for Manual Men

	%
All industries and services	14.1
Agriculture, forestry, and fishing	16.1
Mining and quarrying	15.0
Food, drink and tabacco	20.0
Coal and petroleum products	16.3
Chemicals	14.6
Metal manufacture	11.7
Mechanical engineering	13.9
Instrument engineering	12.0
Electrical engineering	12.2
Shipbuilding and marine engineering	17.2
Vehicles	11.0
Other metal goods	12.5
Textiles	12.6
Clothing and footwear	5.5
Bricks, pottery, glass, cement, etc.	15.5
Timber, furniture, etc.	11.3
Paper, printing and publishing	13.2
Other manufacturing	13.1
Gas, electricity and water	11.3
Transport and communications	20.2
Distributive trades	13.2
Insurance, banking, finance and business services	15.8
Professional and scientific services	11.2
Miscellaneous services	11.2
Public administration	11.4

CHAPTER TEN

Perks and Benefits

Perks or fringe benefits are compensation that comes in addition to basic salaries. The terms are usually associated with white collar work; benefits for manual workers are known as allowances and are dealt with in chapter seven.

Perks account for a substantial percentage of white collar compensation: an average figure of 25 – 30 per cent is usually thought accurate for most white collar work, but it can rise to over 50 per cent for certain jobs in banking – famous for its generous benefits. It is often useful to contrast perks with higher salaries to see why they are so popular. An employer can use perks selectively as an incentive or reward without openly distorting his salary structure. In that sense, it becomes another variable that can be changed to motivate employees. But perks can also be used to benefit the company directly. For example, providing workers with a free home phone makes it easier to find them when they are needed at work.

When employers provide workers with perks that are valued, they become an aid in recruiting and retaining a high-quality labour force. In some cases, there are economies to scale and the employer can provide benefits more cheaply than the workers could purchase them as individuals. This is particularly true of assurance plans.

Of course, most perks are desirable and are valued by employees. The fact that they are sometimes tax exempt or taxed at rates lower than income makes them even more attractive. It is frequently the case, though, that employees cannot use some perks or value them less than their cost to the company. Those employees who already own homes, for example, place little value on the cheap home mortgages which are the main perk in the banking industry. In these case, the employees would prefer having the value as additional salary – even at higher tax rates.

The stature of perks and their distribution throughout the economy may change if they are taxed differently, something that the current government has hinted at doing.

The following perks are common for British executives:

Subsidised Housing
For most people, their home is their major financial asset. It is also a tremendous constraint to moving. It is time-consuming and often expensive to sell when one needs to move. Finding new housing is also a problem, particularly in the South East where the shortage of inexpensive accommodation is often cited as a reason why skilled workers do not migrate there to take new jobs.

The constraint that housing puts on mobility has led companies to provide housing assistance in order to attract new employees. First, employers provide grants for relocation which usually meet all moving expenses and sometimes compensate employees if they should suffer a loss on the sale of their home. Second, many employers offer assistance in finding new accommodation. Third, and most important, some companies provide cheap loans so that their employees can easily afford new housing. This perk is usually offered only by financial companies and it is their major benefit. Some companies let their employees secure their own mortgage elsewhere and then pay them a subsidy — essentially, the difference between their interest payments and those that would be made based on a low interest rate. About 10 per cent of British executives receive some financial assistance with housing costs, most in the form of cheap loans.

By encouraging the employee to make a long-term investment in housing, the company has made it more difficult for them to move. Indeed, some companies reschedule these loans should the employee decide to quit and take work elsewhere. In such cases, there is a clear incentive to stay with the company.

Cars
Company cars are the most visible perks in Britain. Almost three-quarters of all executives have full use of a company car, and, of course, not all of these are Minis. Sales executives are the group most likely to get a car; it is frequently necessary for their work. Allowances are also paid against operating costs. Where no car is provided, companies will usually pay and allowance to cover the employee's use of his own car.

The important point about company cars is that they can usually be used for other than business needs.

Transportation Allowances

Some companies provide assistance in meeting the cost of commuting to work by paying for or providing interest-free loans for season tickets on public transport. This assistance is not offered where a company car is provided, and in general would only apply in Central London. Some firms also run their own buses in which executives can ride to and from work. Whether they would or not is another matter.

Bonuses

Bonuses and profit sharing are important sources of cash income for many British executives. Just under 40 per cent of all executives receive bonuses, and they equal, on average, about 12 per cent salary. Bonuses are usually linked to profits or some measure of business performance. Their value, then, is uncertain year-by-year. The intention is to link the size of the bonus to the employee's performance, creating an incentive to further the company's position. Their value as a percentage of salary rises as one climbs the executive ladder. Indications are that the value of bonuses has fallen since last year because of the reduction in business profits.

Life and Health Assurance

Assurance can either be provided free to the employees or subsidised. 60 per cent of British executives receive free medical assurance, and others receive it at reduced rates. 90 per cent receive free life assurance, the face value of which can vary. Of course, if one should decide to leave a company, the contributions to assurance plans cease. Employees can sometimes loose the equity that has been established for them in life assurance plans, and this gives them a further incentive to stay with the company.

Subsidised Meals

This benefit usually comes in the form of an executive dining room where prices are well below their market value. Some employers will pay for executive's lunches in restaurants; most cover meals when they involve entertaining clients. As many as three-quarters of British executives receive some assistance with their lunch costs. Providing these facilities can cut down on the amount of time that employees spend away from their desks.

Personal Loans

These loans usually come as an advance of salary. The usual ceiling on loans is three month's salary. The rate of interest charged will vary between employers, but it is above the rates charged on in-house, cheap mortgages and below those charged by banks for personal loans. It is not a very common perk. Perhaps 5 per cent of all employees have access to it. In banking, however, it is quite common.

Home Telephones

Company allowances for home telephones began with technical employees as a way of keeping them 'on call' in the event of emergencies at the plant. It has spread to management and executive positions, but one may doubt whether the absence of these allowances would keep many executives from installing home telephones. Companies will usually pay the initial installation fee, some-times contributing toward the monthly charges as well. About one-half of all companies provide some assistance with telephone costs, but the proportion of employees who benefit is low.

Clothing Allowances

Clothing allowances were first paid to those manual workers whose jobs required special

garments - especially safety clothing. The
practice has spread to white collar jobs where
contact with the public is necessary - particularly sales. The allowance usually comes in the
form of an addition to basic pay, to cover
cleaning and pressing charges. Some employers,
however, will pick up the bill for their
executives new clothes, especially if they travel
a great deal.

Company Discounts

These discounts operate in two ways. The first
method is to allow employees to purchase goods
through the company; companies can usually
purchase goods at wholesale prices, passing the
savings on to their workers. Second, large
employers can often arrange discounts for their
employees at local retail outlets. Retailers
offer these discounts hoping that they will be
offset by the increase in new customers. Sometimes, the discounts are offered in exchange for
the company's corporate business.

Professional Fee Allowances

The allowances are usually paid to professional
employees - engineers and architects, for
example, to cover the costs of joining career-
orientated societies. Some companies will also
pay membership fees so that their executives can
join private social clubs.

Marriage Bonuses

This perk is usually given to employees at any
level when they get married. It consists of a
small cash payment or gift.

Educational Trusts

Some employers maintain a fund from which grants
are dispensed to help employees meet the cost of

educating their children. Grants are usually limited to those who need help with the costs of higher education.

Share Option/Share Purchase Plans

These schemes, are in essence a way of buying company stock at a discount. Share option plans permit employees to buy stock in the future at a fixed price. If the price of the stock rises to £10 per share and one has a guaranteed option of buying it at £5 per share, the value of the option can be quite substantial. There is often a limit as to how many shares one can purchase, however. The value of this option rests on the assumption that the price of the stock will rise in the future. Share purchase plans allow employees to purchase stock at a discount as they work. One method is to match the employee's purchase - give them one share for each share they buy. Employees canusualy enroll in a purchasing scheme that will deduct the costs of acquiring stock directly from their pay.

Through these plans, employees can acquire a great deal of equity at a small price. Of course, the employee's financial security is then linked to the company's through the value of its stock. About 7 per cent of executives have access to share option or purchase plans.

Pensions

Pension schemes are becoming more common and more complicated. Almost all companies have pension plans for their executives. Not all pensions are alike, however, and it is worth seeing the ways in which they differ.

Are employees contributions required? Over 70 per cent of the plans surveyed required that employees contribute part of the premium. The usual contribution is between 5 and 7 per cent of one's basic salary.

What determines the money value of the pension? The usual procedure is to base it one one's final salary before retiring (true in 88 per cent of firms). This salary is almost always the highest of one's career with the employer. But final salary is usually taken to mean 'basic salary', before any bonuses or cash benefits are paid. The annual value of the pension is figured as some percentage of one's final salary. In over 75 per cent of the companies surveyed, employees receive one sixtieth of their final salary for each year with the employer. An employee with 40 years of service would, therefore, receive an pension equal to two-thirds of his final salary with the company.

At what age can one retire? In 90 per cent of the plans, the retirement age was 65 years. Some schemes allow one to retire early, but of course the value of the pension would then be less.

Are pension adjusted to increases in the cost of living? More than 80 per cent of the plans surveyed provided some adjustment, but almost none adjusted fully and automatically to changes in the cost of living: pensions in the Civil Service, as many of us are now aware, do adjust fully and automatically.

CHAPTER ELEVEN

Regional Pay Variations

Pay obviously varies by region — even when differences in hours worked are excluded. Of course, this may in part be because the average job in each region differs. Those in the City of London are unlikely to be doing the same jobs as those in the South West. Even for the same jobs, though, there are differences in earnings by region.

Perhaps the best explanation for these variations is that workers are not free to pick up and move to new jobs in different areas. Therefore, the supply of labour does not easily adjust to changes in the number of jobs. Where jobs increase, additional workers are hard to find and wages rise. Where jobs decrease, the supply of available workers increases and wages fall — or at least rise less quickly. The number of jobs in engineering, for example, has undergone a slow decline over the past decade in the West Midlands. Average weekly earnings for manual men in the West Midlands were 7 per cent above the average for Britain in 1970; in 1980, after a steady decline in employment, average earnings were 2 per cent below the British average. Similarly, the highest earnings in 1980 for manuals in mechanical engineering were paid in Scotland, which is probably due to the rapid expansion in industrial activity that came with North Sea Oil.

Earnings clearly differ between regions, but the cost of living in those regions also varies. High wages in London, where prices are high, may not leave workers any better off than they would be with lower wages elsewhere. In order to attract workers to the South East, for example, wages would have to be higher than elsewhere - at least high enough to compensate for the extra costs of living. Regional variations in earnings, therefore, may not indicate whether there are regional variations in standards of living.

Regional Variations in Pay - Full-time Manual Men, All Industries and Services

	Excluding Overtime Influence £ Per Hour	Gross Earnings £ Per Hour	£ Per Week
Great Britain	2.41	2.46	111.70
Great London	2.56	2.60	118.80
Other South East	2.37	2.43	111.40
Combined South East	2.45	2.50	114.70
East Anglia	2.24	2.30	105.50
South West	2.24	2.30	103.10
West Midlands	2.41	2.45	110.10
East Midlands	2.39	2.45	110.80
Yorkshire/ Humberside	2.37	2.48	110.50
North West	2.38	2.43	110.50
North	2.46	2.52	112.40
England	2.40	2.45	111.40
Wales	2.45	2.49	111.30
Scotland	2.35	2.42	112.20

Regional Variations In Pay Full-time Non-Manual
Men, All Industries and Services

	Excluding Overtime Influence £ Per Hour	Gross Earnings £ Per Hour	£ Per Week
Great Britain	3.61	3.61	141.30
Greater London	4.19	4.17	162.30
Other South East	3.58	3.58	141.50
Combined South East	3.91	3.90	152.70
East Anglia	3.38	3.37	131.90
South West	3.41	3.41	132.00
West Midlands	3.37	3.38	131.20
East Midlands	3.29	3.29	130.20
Yorkshire/ Humberside	3.37	3.37	132.40
North West	3.45	3.45	136.20
North	3.47	3.45	134.80
England	3.63	3.63	141.80
Wales	3.40	3.41	132.50
Scotland	3.53	3.52	139.60

Average earnings per hour including the influence
of overtime are actually less than average
earnings excluding overtime. The reason is that
non-manuals are rarely paid more for overtime;
their total earnings remain constant, but total
hours rise. Earnings per hour, therefore,
decline.

CHAPTER TWELVE

Are Men Paid More?

<u>MEN AND WOMEN'S PAY VARIATIONS</u>

Do women earn less than men? On average, the answer is quite clearly yes. The average female manual worker's weekly earnings are 40 per cent less than her male colleagues'. The figure is about the same for non-manuals (42 per cent). The question is, how much of this difference can be explained by differences in hours and in jobs? And how much is discrimination — lower pay for the same jobs or for work of equal value?

Manual men work longer hours than manual women, and that increases their weekly earnings and their average hourly earnings, the latter because of overtime premiums rates. But if one looks at hourly pay excluding the influence of overtime premiums, a gap between men's and women's pay remains. Average hourly earnings for men are £2.38 versus £1.71 for women.

Figures in the first chart have averaged across all manual jobs in the various industries. There is no reason to believe that the 'average' job held by women in an industry is the same a the 'average' job held by men. Throughout this book, one comes across jobs that are low skill, lack union representation and are low paid. A great many of these involve part-time and homework. Women are disproportionately represented in these jobs - cleaning, garment and textile work, low grade clerical, etc. It is interesting, although beyond the scope of this book, to ask why women should be over-represented in these jobs. The answers, it would seem have everything to do with social attitudes: the demands families make on women's time, the types of education and careers thought to be appropriate and so on. It is also interesting to ask whether those jobs would be low paid if they were dominated by men. There are examples of low-skilled, predominately male occupations that pay quite well, e.g. dockers. The difference here is a strong union. But then, one might ask, why are there not strong unions for jobs dominated by women.

The remaining explanation for sex differential in pay is discrimination which is just another way of saying that it is not due to differences in jobs, output or hours. The Sex Discrimination Act of 1975 establishes the right of women to equal treatment in terms of pay and other conditions of employment

> 'when she is employed on work of the same nature as, or which is broadly similar to, that of a man...and there is no material difference of sex between her case and his.'

This comparison between the treatment of the sexes can only be made for jobs, with the same employer, however. According to the act, discrimination by an employer is illegal. Of course, this doesn't mean that it never happens. And it does not make discrimination between employers illegal. For example, a contract cleaning firm whose employees are entirely female can send its workers into a plant to work alongside the plant's janitors - who are all male. The janitors can earn twice as much as the cleaners, but because the employers are different, the Sex Discrimination Act does not apply.

The following set of tables, highlights the difference in earnings for male and female employees in the same general occupations. Men earn more here, too, but it is impossible to say that the actual jobs in which the two sexes are employed are identical. Even if they were exactly identical, there might be differences in output-related earnings, seniority, all of which are relevant to pay and do not constitute discrimination.

Comparing the two charts, the gap between men's and women's earnings is less by occupation than by industry group. To the extent that jobs are more or less similar in the latter (at least more so than in the former), this comparison indicates – as one would expect – that part of the earnings gap is due to differences in occupations. It would be difficult to estimate how much is due to discrimination as prohibited in the Act. One might hazard a guess, though, and say that a more important source of discrimination is that which governs the selection of careers.

Pay Differences Between Men and Women by Occupation 1980 – New Earnings Survey 1980 Men Earn This Much More:

Non-Manual	£ Per Hour (Earnings)	£ Per Week (Earnings)	% Weekly
Management and administration		46.5	72
Teachers in establishments of further education		26.3	83

Non-Manual	£ Per Hour (Earnings)	£ Per Week (Earnings)	% Weekly
Secondary teachers		16.1	87
Primary teacher		17.9	85
Other teachers		20.8	83
Welfare workers		26.1	79
Nurse administrators and executives		22.9	84
Registered nurses and midwives		16.2	83
Literary, artistic and sports		43.9	70
Science, engineering and technology		50.5	65
Laboratory technicians	.62	27.3	75
Office managers		55.3	67
Hotel, club or public house manager		23.2	76
Supervisor of clerks	.50	21.3	83
Finance, Insurance, etc. clerks	.62	26.1	73
ADP processing operators	.99	45.6	62
Telephonists	.27	32.1	68
Sales supervisor	.77	39.5	65
Salesperson, shop assistant	.73	35.0	61
Security and protective service	.48	30.0	78
Manual			
Catering supervisors	.48	32.8	69

Manual	£ Per Hour (Earnings)	£ Per Week (Earnings)	% Weekly
Chefs/cooks	.37	33.9	66
Bar persons	.28	25.6	69
Kitchen hands	.33	24.6	69
Supervisors/ cleaning, caretaking, etc.	.44	28.3	80
Other cleaners	.38	25.9	70
Materials processing (excluding metals)	.79	44.8	58
Making and repairing (excluding metals & electric)	.82	44.2	59
Footwear workers	.54	25.3	72
Machine tool operators	.65	32.4	69
Press and stamping machine operators	.91	40.0	62
Repetitive assemblers	.57	27.8	71
Inspectors and testers	.80	41.5	64
Packers, canners and fillers	.54	35.1	65
Transport, moving & storage	.48	31.1	71
Storekeepers,etc	.35	23.2	75

Summary			
All non-manual occupations	1.39	58.4	58
Manual occupations	.73	42.7	61
All occupations	.81	44.2	64

Pay Differentials Between Men and Women by
Industry - 1980 New Earnings Survey 1981 by
Occupations and by Industry

	£ Per Hour (Earnings)	£ Per Week (Earnings)	% Weekly
All industries and services	1.39	58.4	58
Industries producing/ processing food	1.52	63.6	54
Industries producing/ processing drink	1.61	63.5	55
General Chemicals	2.27	87.1	50
Iron and Steel	1.59	64.2	53
Other machinery	1.54	67.9	51
Instrument engineering	1.62	66.6	53
Radio, radar & electronics	1.49	65.0	53
Motor vehicle manufacturing	1.48	66.3	54
Aerospace	1.50	61.8	57
Textile production	1.77	73.9	47
Clothing		58.6	
Brick and glass manufacturing	1.40	58.6	55
Furniture manufacturing	1.42	63.0	51
Printing and publishing	1.40	62.9	58
Bookbinding and engraving	1.79	51.9	56

	£ Per Hour (Earnings)	£ Per Week (Earnings)	% Weekly
Construction	1.51	65.0	51
Gas, electricity and water	1.76	72.0	54
Air transport	1.64	76.7	58
Postal and telecommunications	0.97	45.3	65
Transport and storage	1.48	66.2	52
Wholesale distribution	1.54	63.3	54
Retail distribution	1.12	48.9	55

Pay Differential Between Men and Women by Industry 1980 - Men Earn This Much More:

	£ Per Hour	£ Per Week	% Weekly
Coal, oil, grain and agriculture	1.09	51.3	55
Industrial materials & machinery	1.37	64.6	51
Insurance	2.22	83.9	47
Banking and bill discount	2.25	79.2	50
Other financial institutions	1.94	73.4	51
Other business services	1.63	71	53
Central offices	1.77	73.8	55
Accountancy services	1.26	47.7	61
Educational services	.87	31.5	77
Legal services	1.36	47.8	58

	£ Per Hour	£ Per Week	% Weekly
Medical and dental services	1.38	60.3	59
Research and development	1.43	54.7	64
Other professional services	1.53	63.6	55
Catering	.59	29.2	70
Motor repairs, filling stations	1.05	55.7	53
National government services	1.33	59.3	61
Local government services	1.31	57.2	59

CHAPTER THIRTEEN

Are The Old Paid Less?

DISTRIBUTION OF EARNINGS BY AGE GROUPS

The first thing one notices about the charts comparing wages to age groups is that young workers are the lowest paid. The reason is first, that in many occupations, basic rates are lower for young employees, reflecting the fact that they are learning the job and are as yet unskilled. Second, even where basic rates are the same, young workers are often given the most basic and lowest-paying-jobs in the heirarchy. This is almost always the case in non-manual work.

It is also apparent that young manuals earn more than their non-manual counterparts. In part, this is because manuals work longer hours, but many argue that manual skills take less time to acquire and therefore that young manuals become productive workers more quickly. The position is decisively reversed at the 25 year band for men and the 21 year band for women, ages when those who have education and technical training enter the non- manual labour force.

Earnings seem to rise for each age group. Yet, the older workers actually seem to be earning less than those just a few years younger. It is important to note that these charts are a cross-section of the labour force in 1980 and in no way represent the experience of any individual in their lifetime.

Rapid increases come up through the middle of a career; specific skills and training are acquired, promotions and job changes move one rapidly up the salary scale. As retirement approaches, however, promotions taper off and salary grades remain more or less constant. Earnings do not decline.

Why is it, then, that workers in these older age groups earn less than their younger counterparts? Some of the difference may be because younger employees particularly manuals work longer hours. But the gap remain even when one looks at basic hourly earnings. From occupational surveys it is clear that older workers do not earn less than younger ones in the same jobs. The difference, therefore, must be because older workers, on average, are in occupations that pay less than those held by slightly younger workers. They move to these occupations, because they are less taxing and strenuous.

| | Median Earnings | |
| | £ Per Week | |
Manuals	Men	Women
Under 18	45.50	45.00
18–20	73.40	58.30
21–24	94.20	65.30
25–29	103.70	68.10
30–39	111.20	67.60
40–49	110.00	66.40
50–59	103.30	64.80
60–64	95.20	59.90
65 and over	88.80	58.70

Non-Manuals	Median Earnings £ Per Week Men	Women
Under 18	44.60	42.80
18-20	65.70	57.90
21-24	88.80	71.60
25-29	113.70	83.90
30-39	136.20	85.50
40-49	143.70	83.60
50-59	134.00	81.80
60-64	117.00	78.60
65 and over	118.90	72.60

How Weekly Wages Compare

NEW EARNINGS SURVEY 1980
Occupations Ranked by Average Weekly Earnings

Non-Manuals	£ per week
Medical Practitioners	242.20
Finance, Insurance, tax, specialists	209.60
University Academic Staff	205.70
Police Inspectors and above, Fire Service Officers	196.80
Prison Officers below Principal Officer	191.70
Personnel and Industrial Relations Officers	185.50
Marketing and Sales Managers	183.20
Company Secretaries	178.90
Ships Officers	178.10
Supervisors (Police Sergeants, Fire Fighting, etc.)	172.90
Journalists	172.50
Advertising and PR Managers	171.40
Office Managers	169.10
General Administrators – Local Government	166.80
Architects and Town Planners	166.00

	£ per week
Engineers – Electrical	165.20
Scientists and Mathematicians	164.20
Production and Works Managers, Works Foremen	163.30
Engineers – Mechanical	160.10
Engineers – Civil	157.40
Systems Analysts, Computer Programmers	157.30
Accountants	157.10
Work, Study etc., Officers	155.20
Teachers in Establishments for Further Education	154.40
Metallurgists and Other Technologists	150.70
Public Health Inspectors	150.50
Engineering Maintenance Managers	149.60
Engineers – Production	147.00
Engineers – Planning	147.00
Buyers	146.50
Transport Managers	146.20
Nurse Administrators	144.00
Policemen (below Sergeant)	142.20
Distribution Managers	140.70
Site Managers, Clerks of Works, General Foremen	140.00
Industrial Designers	139.90
Industrial Trainers	139.40
Building, Land, Mining Surveyors	137.90
Quantity Surveyors	132.90
Engineering Technicians,	132.30
Other Sales Representatives and Agents	129.70
Technical Sales Representatives	128.80
Warehouseing Managers	128.40
Draughtsmen	128.40
Secondary Teachers	125.30

	£ per week
Welfare Workers	124.80
Supervisors of Clerks	124.70
Primary Teachers	123.50
Planning Assistants and Building Technicians	122.60
Store Managers	121.90
Security Officers and Detectives	118.80
Firemen	118.40
Security Guards	115.20
Branch Managers of Shops	112.90
Sales Supervisors	112.20
Laboratory Technicians	112.00
Sales Representatives (wholesale goods	109.30
Roundsmen and Van Salesmen	106.20
Postmen, Messengers	105.50
Telephonists	104.30
Shipping and Travel Clerks	104.00
Hotel, Catering, Club or Pub Managers	98.70
Finance, Insurance, Clerks	98.40
Managers of Independent Shops (employees)	98.30
Registered and Enrolled Nurses and Midwives	97.80
Cash Handling Clerks	97.60
Production and Materials Controlling Clerks	96.60
General Clerks and Clerks	96.30
Costing and Accounting Clerks	93.10
Records and Library Clerks	91.20
Salesmen, Shop Assistants, Shelf Fillers	90.30

Occupations Ranked by Average Weekly Earnings
Manual

	£ per week
Deputies - coalmining	177.80
Foremen - Chemical Processing	154.90
Face-trained Coalminers	253.60
Foremen, Electrical Installation and Maintenance	150.00
Foremen - Metal Pipes, Sheets, etc.	148.10
Stevedores and Dockers	146.50
Steel Erection, Scaffolders, Steelbenders, Fixers	141.80
Foremen -Machine Install ation and Maintenance	139.30
Electricity Power Plant Operators, Switchboard Attendants	138.20
Foremen - Production Fitting (metal)	136.40
Foremen - Metal Making and Treating	135.90
Deck and Engine Room Hands	134.10
Electricians - Installation and Maintenance, Plant	133.60
Printing, Paper Making	133.00
Foremen - Engineering, Machining	132.80
Compositors	132.00
Gas Fitters	131.60
Foremen - Product Inspect ion and Repetitive Assembly	131.50
Printing Machine Minders	131.20
Ambulance Men	129.80
Maintenance Fitters (non-electrical)	128.70

	£ per week
Electricians – Installation and Maintenance – Premises and Ships	127.40
Foremen Building and Civil Engineering	125.80
Chemical, Gas, etc. Plant Operators	125.50
Foremen – Transport	125.10
Foremen – Food and Drink Processing	123.90
Crane Drivers/Operators	123.60
Toolmakers, Tool Fitters	122.50
Welders (skilled)	121.80
Production Fitters (electrical/electronic)	121.40
Heating and Ventilating Engineering Fitters	121.00
Platers and Metal Shipwrights	120.70
Printing Machine Assistants	120.70
Heavy Goods Drivers	120.10
Plumbers, Pipe Fitters	118.60
Foremen – Woodworking	118.60
Inspectors and Testers Metal and Electrical	117.50
Bus and Coach Drivers	117.40
Maintenance and Installation Fitters	117/10
Metal Working Production Fitters (fine limits)	116.10
Machine – Toolsetter-Operators	115.70
Sheet Metal Workers	115.20
Locomotive Drivers, Motormen	115.20
Railway Signalmen and Shunters	114.40

	£ per week
Fettlers/Dressers	114.10
Other Centre Lathe Turners	113.80
Coach and Vehicle Body Builders/Makers	113.50
Foremen – Materials Moving and Storing	113.30
Other Metal–Working Production Fitters (not to fine limits)	113.10
Mechanical Plant Drivers/ Operators (civil engin- eering)	112.90
Moulders, Coremakers, Diemasters	112.60
Press and Machine Tool Setters	112.10
Layers, Pipe Joiners and Sewermen (maintenance)	111.80
Carpenters and Joiners	111.20
Viewers (metal and electrical)	110.90
Cable Joiners and Linesmen	110.90
Machine Tool Operator (not setting up)	110.60
Press and Stamping Machine Operators	110.30
Coach Painters, other Spray Painters	110.00
Fork Lift Operators	109.30
Bricklayers	109.00
Motor Vehicle Mechanics (skilled)	108.20
Cabinet Case and Box Makers	107.60
Moulding Machine Operators (rubber plastics)	107.40
Catering Supervisors	106.90
Telephone Fitters	106.20

	£ per week
Maintenance Fitters/ Mechanics – Radio, TV etc.	106.20
Carpenters, Joiners, Building and Maintenance	105.90
Railway Trackmen and Plate Layers	104.80
Bus Conductors	104.60
Supervisors, Foremen – Caretaking, Cleaning, etc	104.30
Other Motor Drivers	103.50
Packers, Bottlers, Canners	102.20
Roadmen	101.70
Repetitive Assemblers	101.40
Civil Engineering Labourers	100.50
Refuse Collectors, Dustmen	99.90
Other Motor Vehicle Mechanics	99.50
Woodworking Machinists and	99.40
Goods Porters	99.10
Painters and Decorators	98.90
Chefs/Cooks	98.40
Bakers/Confectioners	98.20
Plasters	98.10
Railmen, Stationmen	97.10
Hospital Porters	96.90
Footwear Workers	94.70
Store Keepers, etc.	94.50
Other Goods Drivers	94.10
General Labourers (including engineering and shipbuilding)	94.00
Craftsmen Mates, Building Labourers, etc.	93.60
Bleachers, Dyers, Finishers	92.40
Stockmen	91.50
Agricultural Machinery Drivers/Operators	90.50

	£ per week
Caretakers	90.40
Other Cleaners	89.70
Gardeners and Groundsmen	86.70
Roadsweepers	82.90
Butchers, Meat Cutters	82.90
Barmen	80.40
Kitchen Hands	80.40
General Farmworkers	80.10

Sources of House-hold Income

SOURCES OF THE AVERAGE HOUSEHOLD INCOME

Wages and salaries are not the only sources of household income. As one can see from the following chart, however, they are far and away the most important source, especially as the level of insurance and pension benefits depends on employment earnings. But a chart like this cannot indicate the distribution of these different types of income within the society. Most households receive almost no rent, dividend or interest payments, for example, but for some they are the entire source of income – often quite a high level of income.

Types of Income and Distribution

	%
Wages and Salaries	60.0
Cash payment to HM Forces	1.0
Self-employment income	9.5
Net rent, dividends and interest	2.0
Pensions, life assurance, superann-uation schemes and other benefits	18.0
National Insurance and other contrib-utions from employers	4.5
Income in kind	1.0
Rent from owner-occupied dwellings	4.0
	100.0

APPENDIX THREE

1924 v 1980 Wages Compared

COMPARISON OF WAGES IN CERTAIN OCCUPATIONS
1924 v. 1980

	1924	1980
	£ per week	
Bakers	3.20	98.20
Cobblers	3.00	94.70
Building Industry		
(a) Craftsmen	3.68	109.60
(b) Labourers	2.78	93.60
Electricity Installers	3.76	127.40
Engineering Labourers	2.00	100.50
Firemen	2.63	118.40
Furniture Makers	3.72	210.80
Local Authorities' Services	2.65	146.10
Printing Compositors	3.70	132.00
Railway trackmen	2.45	104.80

List of Acknowledgements

For material in the book and for help in my researches I would like to thank the following: Remuneration Economics Ltd and the British Institute of Management, the Low Pay Unit, the Council of Engineering Institutions, *Selection* and *Building* magazines, the Institute of Sales Management, the Royal Society of Chemists.

Many HMSO publications have been a help to me but I would like to acknowledge in particular: New Earnings Survey, Inland Revenue Statistics, Time Rates of Wages and Hours of Work, National Income and Expenditure, Standing Commission on Pay Comparability Reports, Salary Review Body Reports and the Department of Employment *Gazette*.

My thanks must also go to: Rob Bell, Michael Dixon, Joe Clark, Jane Trewhella, John Wright, Andrew Schuller, Carol O'Brien and Julian Watson along with special thanks to Barbara Roberts who undertook the most difficult research with remarkable efficiency.

Index

Accountancy, 63
Advertising, 123–4
  account executive, 123
  art directors, 124
  copywriters, 124
  marketing manager, brand/
    product manager, 123
  traffic/production executive,
    124
Aerated water workers, 142
Air transport workers, 159–60
Airline personnel, 177–9
  cabin crew, 178–9
  co-pilot, 177
  flight engineer, 177–8
  pilot-in-command, 177
Airport fuel truck driver, 180
Ambulancemen, 48–9
Architects, 55–6
Armed forces, 33–9
  senior officers in the, 33–4
Army, 36–7
Artificial flower makers, *see*
  Ostrich and feather and
  artificial flower makers
Artificial limb makers, 148
Artists, 73–4
  industrial, 85
Atomic energy workers, 163
Authorised clerk, 60
Automobile club staff, 187
Auxiliary medical professions,
  47–8
  chiropodist, 47
  dietitian, 48
  occupational therapists, 47
  orthoptist, 48
  physiotherapist, 47
  radiographer, 48
  remedial gymnast, 47
  speech therapist, 48

Baking, 143–4
Banking, 115–19
  assistant managers, 116
  banking advisors, 119
  bond dealers, 118
  bond issue managers, 120

branch managers, 116
corporate finance executives, 117
documentary credit managers, 114–15
financial controllers, 121
foreign exchange dealers, 117
foreign exchange/money managers, 116
general manager, 115
investment fund portfolio manager, 119
loan managers, 116
project finance directors, 117
senior lending officers, 117
syndication managers, 118
Barristers/solicitors, 56–9
Bespoke shoemakers/repairers, 148
Blacksmiths, 137
Book publishing, 84–5
Broom makers, see Brush and broom makers
Brush and broom makers, 153
Building, 134–5
Bureau de change, 120
Bus conductors, see Bus drivers and conductors
Bus drivers and conductors, 180–1
Butchers/slaughtermen, 143
Button makers, 154
Buyers (wholesale/retail), 124–5

Cabinet makers, see Furniture makers
Careers officers, 29
Carpet makers, 152–3

Catering, 91–2
Ceramic workers, 154–5
Chauffeurs, 179
Chemical workers, 155–6
Chemists, 170–1
China workers, see Pottery/china workers, 155
Cinema workers, 81
Circus performers, 77–8
Civil servants, 19
Cleaners, 96
Clergy, 51–4
Baptists, 53
Episcopal Church of Scotland, 54
Methodist, 54
Roman Catholic, 57
Unitarian and free churches, 53
United Reformed Church, 54–5
Wesleyan Reform Union, 54
Clerical work, 111–3
temporary, 113
Clothing, 149–51
corset makers, 159–50
dressmaking and women's light clothing, 149
glove makers, 150
hat, cap and millinery, 151
ready-made and wholesale bespoke tailoring, 149
retail bespoke tailoring, 150–1
shirt, collar and tie, wholesale mantle and costume corset manufacturing, 149
Coal miners, 131
Coffin and cerement workers, 192
College/university manual

staff, 95
Computing workers, 168–9
Confectionary, *see* Sugar,
    confectionary, cocoa and
    chocolate makers,
Coopers, 140
Counsellers, 191
Cricketers, 88–9
Cutlery and silverware workers,
    157–8

Dancers, 76–7
Dental technicians, 44
Dentists, *see* Doctors and
    dentists
Depot or warehouse manager,
    see Distribution specialists
Designers, industrial, 85
Directors, 99–103
Distribution specialists, 111
Divers, 183–4
Dockers/stevedores, 159
Doctors and dentists, 41–2
Doormen, 93–4
Draughtsmen, 87

Economists, 62
Embalmers, 192
Employment agents, 114
Engineering, 131–4
Engineers, 68–71
Escalator erectors, *see* Lift and
    escalator erectors
Estate agents, 64
Exhibition craftsmen, 190–1

Farm labour, 138–9
Fellmongering, 144–5
Film developers, 156
Fire service, 24

Flour milling, 142–3
Footballers, 87–8
Football managers, 88
Foremen, *see* Supervisors/
    foremen
Forestry workers, 136
Funeral workers, 191–2
Furniture makers, 140–1

Gardeners/groundsmen, 139
Gas technicians, 185
Girl/guy Friday, 114
Government, 16
    ministers, 17–18
    top salaries in, 15–18
Government scientists, 39–40
Groundsmen, *see* Gardeners/
    groundsmen

Hairdressing, 175–6
Head-hunters/personnel
    consultants, 121–2
Heating and ventilation
    workers, 135
Hide and skin traders, 145
Home economists, 97
Horse racing, 89–90
    jockeys, 89
    owners, 89–90
    stable lads, 89
Hotels, 92–3
    bar staff, 93
    chambermaids, 93
    doormen, 93–4
    hall porters, 93
    head receptionists, head
    housekeepers, 93
Housekeepers, 97
House of Commons, 16–18
House of Lords, 17–18

Import/export manager, see Distribution specialists
Industrial civil servants, 19–20
Industrial designers, 85
Industrial manufacture, 146
Industrial medical officers/ occupational physicians, 45
Industrial relations officers/ specialists, 65–6
Insolvency experts, see Receivership/insolvency experts
Inspector, see Verifier/ inspector
Insurance, 62
International traders, 61
Interpreter, see Translator/ interpreter
Investment advisor, 60
Investment analyst, 60

Jobber, see Stockjobber
Journalists, 82
  in commercial radio, 82
Judiciary, 29–32

Key punch operators, 169
Lace makers, 151–2
Leather goods manufacturer, 146
Leather/wool/animal skins, 144
Librarians, 85
Lift and escalator erectors, 135–6
Linen finishers, 151
Local authority workers, 22–3
  clerical, 23
  manual, 22–3
Local government worker, see Local authority workers

Lock, latch and key makers, 137
Locksmiths, 137–8
Lollipop men or women, see School crossing attendants

Maintenance craftsmen, 161–2
Make-up artist, 76
Malt distilling, 147
Management consultants, 65
Managers, 103–7
  accounting, 104–5
  advertising, 104
  company secretary, 107
  corporate planning, 104
  distribution, see Distribution specialists
  investment/capital projects, 104
  personnel, 107
  production, 105–6
  public relations, 107
  purchasing, 105
  quality control, 107
  research, 108
  research and development, 105
  sales, 105
Manual workers, 127–9
  perks (allowances) for, 129–31
Marketing analysts, 124
Match makers, 142
Mechanics, see Motor vehicle mechanics
Merchant navy/sea transport, 182–3
Messengers, 187
Metallurgists, 169–60
Metro workers, 181

Midwives, *see* Nurses/
  midwives
Miners, *see* Coal miners
Models, 176–7
Motor vehicle mechanics, 161
Musicians, 74–5

Nationalised industries, 20–2
Newsagents, 190
New towns staff, 40
Nurses/midwives, 44–5

Occupational physicians, *see*
  Industrial medical officers
Off-licence staff, 94
Oil rig workers, 185–5
Operations research, 122
  manager, 122–3
Organ building, *see* Pianoforte
  manufacture/organ building
Ostrich and feather and
  artificial flower makers, 152

Parliament, 15–18
Pension fund managers, 61
Personnel consultants, *see*
  Head-hunter/personnel
  consultants
Personnel managers, 107
Pharmacists, 171–2
Photographers, 78–9
Physicists, 170
Pianoforte manufacture/organ
  building, 141–2
Police, 25
Post office workers, 158
Potters/china workers, 155
Power engineers/electrical
  supply, 162–3
Press officer, *see* Publicity

officer/press officer
Printers, 156–7
Prison officers, 26
Private investigator, 167–8
Probation officers, 26
Psychologists, 46–7
  clinical, 47
  occupational, 47
Publicity officer/press officer,
  125
Publishing, *see* Book publishing

Radio staff, 81
Railwaymen, 181
Receivership/insolvency
  experts, 61
Researchers, 121–2
Retail sales, 110–11
  driver-salesmen/van
    salesmen 110–11
  roundsmen, 110
  salesmen/shop assistants 110
Royal Air Force, 38–9
Royal family, 165–6
Royal Marines, 35
Royal Navy and Royal Marines,
  34–5
Rugby footballers, 88

Saddlers, 147
Sales representatives/
  executives, 107–9
School crossing attendants, 190
School meals personnel, 96–5
Sea transport, *see* Merchant
  navy
Secretarial workers, *see*
  Clerical work
Security/protection employees,
  166–7

hotel detectives, 167
security officer/watchman, 167
store detectives, 167
Senior grades of the higher civil service, 18
Senior officers in the armed forces, 33–5
Ship masters, 182
Shop assistants, 173–4
Shop or store managers, *see* Shop assistants

Silver workers, *see* Cutlery and silverware workers
Slaughtermen, *see* Butchers/slaughtermen
Social work, 26–9
    child-care workers, 27
    community leisure officer, 28
    family social workers, 27–8
    houseparents, 27
    housing manager, 29
    occupational therapist, 28–9
    play leaders, 27
    senior social worker, 28
    sports coach, 28
    training officer, 28
    youth leaders, 27
Solicitors, *see* Barristers/solicitors
Statisticians, 120–1
Steeplejacks, 136
Stevedores, *see* Dockers/stevedores
Stockbroker, 59
Stockjobber, 59–60
Stockroom workers, 158
Students, 188–9

Sugar confectionery, cocoa, and chocolate makers, 143
Supervisors/foremen, 157
Surveyors, 186

Tanners, curriers and dressers, 145
Tax consultants, 59
Taxi drivers, 179–80
Teachers, 66–7
    university, 67
Television, 79–80
Temporary clerical workers, 113
Theatre, 75–6
Time and motion officers, *see* Operations research
Top salaries in government, 15–18
Translator/interpreter, 114–15
Transport engineer, *see* Distribution specialists
Tree surgeons, 140

University teachers, 67
University technicians, 169

Valuer, 64
Vehicle construction, 160–1
Verifier/inspector, 187
Veterinary surgeons, 49

Warehouse workers, 146
Waterways staff, 183
Window dressers, 175
Women's Royal Air Force, 38
Women's Royal Army Corps, 37–8
Women's Royal Navy, 36
Work study manager, *see* Operations research

All Futura Books are available at your bookshop or newsagent, or can be ordered from the following address:
Futura Books, Cash Sales Department,
P.O. Box 11, Falmouth, Cornwall.

Please send cheque or postal order (no currency), and allow 40p for postage and packing for the first book plus 18p for the second book and 13p for each additional book ordered up to a maximum charge of £1.49 in U.K.

Customers in Eire and B.F.P.O. please allow 40p for the first book, 18p for the second book plus 13p per copy for the next 7 books, thereafter 7p per book.

Overseas customers please allow 60p for postage and packing for the first book and 18p per copy for each additional book.